MAKE EVERY
SECOND COUNT

TIME MANAGEMENT TIPS AND TECHNIQUES
FOR MORE SUCCESS WITH LESS STRESS

By Robert W. Bly

CAREER
PRESS

Pompton Plains, NJ

Copyright © 2010 by Robert Bly

MAKE EVERY SECOND COUNT
EDITED BY JODI BRANDON
TYPESET BY NICOLE DEFELICE
Cover design by Jeff Piasky
Printed in the U.S.A.

To order this title, please call toll-free 1-800-CAREER-1 (NJ and Canada: 201-848-0310) to order using VISA or MasterCard, or for further information on books from Career Press.

The Career Press, Inc.
220 West Parkway, Unit 12
Pompton Plains, NJ 07444
www.careerpress.com

Library of Congress Cataloging-in-Publication Data

Bly, Robert W.
    Make every second count : time management tips and techniques for more success with less stress / by Robert Bly.
        p. cm.
    Includes bibliographical references and index.
        ISBN 978-1-60163-133-6 -- ISBN 978-1-60163-716-1
(ebook) 1. Time management. I. Title.

HD69.T54B63 2011
650.1'1--dc22

                                          2010044128

Dedication

To Jodi Van Valkenburg

Acknowledgments

Thanks to the staff at Career Press for publishing the first edition of this book, and then giving me the delightful task of updating it 10 years later.

Contents

Introduction   7

Chapter 1: Work Habits That Speed You Up   13

Chapter 2: Do You Really Want to Be Productive?   33

Chapter 3: Goal-Setting   51

Chapter 4: Save Time and Money When You Travel   61

Chapter 5: The 10% Solution for Increased Personal Efficiency   71

Chapter 6: Networking Online   87

Chapter 7: Using Technology to Save Time   103

Chapter 8: Going Mobile   117

Chapter 9: Delegation and Outsourcing 133

Chapter 10: Getting Organized 151

Chapter 11: Planning Systems and Software to Increase
Your Productivity 167

Chapter 12: Maximizing Your Personal Energy 179

Chapter 13: Managing Information Overload 193

Chapter 14: Saving Time at Home 207

Index 219

About the Author 223

INTRODUCTION

"You may delay, but Time will not."
—Benjamin Franklin, American statesman and philosopher

I'm looking at my watch. It's 8:38 on a Friday morning. By my calculations, assuming I live to age 75, I have only approximately 201,480 hours of life left. I intend to make the most of the time still available to me. How about you?

Today, the demands on our time are tremendous. Everyone has too much to do and not enough time to do it. According to an article in *Men's Health* magazine, 42 percent of American workers believe they are overloaded with work.

We live in the Age of Now. Customers are more demanding than ever. They want everything yesterday. As *The Miami Herald* columnist Leonard Pitts comments, "We move faster than ever, but never quite fast enough."

"When our society travels at electronic speed, we fall under the sway of a new force...the power of now," says Stephen Bertman, a professor at the University of Windsor. "It replaces duration with immediacy, permanence with transience, memory with sensation, insight with impulse." He argues that this acceleration of change contributes to "a growing sense of stress, disorientation, and loss." On the other hand, if you master strategies for coping with today's accelerated pace, you can meet the demands placed upon you while still having time for yourself.

According to an article in *American Demographics,* consumers have come to view time as their most precious commodity: "To satisfy today's consumer, you need to do business in a real-time world—one in which time and distance collapse, action and response are simultaneous, and customers demand instant gratification."

"We've learned to live by the Rule of 6," notes Gary Springer in an article in the *Business-to-Business Marketer.* "What used to take six months, now takes six weeks; what used to take six weeks now is wanted in six days; what normally took six days is needed in six hours; and what used to be done in six hours is now expected in six minutes." Technology, says Springer, is responsible for much of this impatience.

Downsizing has left organizations leaner and meaner. Thousands of workers have been laid off, and those who remain must take up the slack and are working harder than ever. According to a Harris poll, the average work week increased from 41 to 50 hours between 1973 and 1993.

A radio commercial for Bigelow Herbal Tea observes, "We seem to live our lives in perpetual motion." In fact, we're so busy, we don't even have time to eat: The "lunch hour" is fast disappearing from the American business world as workers more frequently eat lunch at their desks. The article "Shrinking Lunch Hours" in *The Futurist* tells us that 40 percent of workers take no lunch break at all and the typical lunch break is 36 minutes, although many people use that time to take care of personal business rather than eat. Recently I read that cereal sales are declining because cereal and milk can't be eaten in the car while driving; breakfast bars meet that need better.

In *The Worst Years of Our Lives* (HarperPerennial), Barbara Ehrenreich writes:

> I don't know when the cult of conspicuous busyness began, but it has swept up almost all the upwardly mobile, professional women I know. Already, it is getting hard to recall the days when, for example, "Let's have lunch," meant something other than, "I've got more important things to do than talk to you right now." There was even a time when people used to get together without the excuse of needing to eat something—when, in fact, it was considered rude to talk with your mouth full. In the old days, hardly anybody had an appointment book....
>
> It's not only women, of course; for both sexes, busyness has become an important insignia of upper-middle-class status. Nobody, these days, admits to having a hobby, although two or more careers—say, neurosurgery and an art dealership—is not uncommon, and I am sure we will soon be hearing more about the tribulations of the four-paycheck couple....

You can't jam 25 hours into a 24-hour day. Time is a nonrenewable resource that's consumed at a constant and relentless rate. Once an hour is gone, it's gone forever; you can never get it back.

Yet you can solve most of your time-related problems—not enough time, too much to do, deadlines too short, bosses too demanding, not getting to your own priorities—simply by increasing the productivity of the one resource you can control: you. As management consultant Stephen Covey notes, "The only person over whom you have direct and immediate control is yourself."

Some human resources professionals refer to the people in their organizations as "resources." That's cold, but, in a way, appropriate and accurate. You are a resource. You have output. To succeed today, you need to increase your output to the next level without making the resource sick, tired, dissatisfied, or unhappy. That's where this book can help.

Make Every Second Count shows you how to succeed in today's competitive, fast-paced world by increasing your own personal productivity, so you can get more done in less time. Going beyond conventional time management, *Make Every Second Count* offers diverse strategies and tactics to empower you to gain this productivity boost—everything from planning, scheduling, organizing, and eliminating time-wasters, to suggestions on improving life habits that give you more energy so you can work better and faster, to using the latest technology to manage information and communicate more efficiently and effectively.

After reading this book you will be better equipped to:

- Get more done in less time.
- Meet deadlines and commitments.
- Have time left over for the things you really want to do.
- Increase customer satisfaction.
- Enhance your on-the-job performance.
- Have more time for family, personal, and other important activities.
- Feel better and have more energy.
- Eliminate time-wasters.
- Benefit from the latest time-saving technologies.
- Improve your efficiency.
- Find the information you need easier and faster.
- Reduce pressure and stress.
- Get through your work backlog.

Make Every Second Count is organized into 14 quick-reading chapters. Six of these chapters are new and have been added to this second edition: goal setting (Chapter 3), saving time when you travel (Chapter 4), networking online (Chapter 6), mobile communication (Chapter 8), planning systems (Chapter 11), and saving time at home (Chapter 14). Several others, in particular the one on using technology to save time (Chapter 7), have been substantially updated and revised.

English author Samuel Butler called time "the only true purgatory," and Ralph Waldo Emerson said time is "the surest poison." I disagree. How you use your time is largely up to you. *Make Every Second Count* shows you how to transform time from an enemy into an ally—and become the master of your time, rather than its slave. The best time to start? Right now.

I do have one favor to ask. If you have a personal productivity technique that works for you, why not send it to me so I can share it with readers of the next edition of this book? You will receive full credit, of course. Contact me at:

Bob Bly

Center for Technical Communication

590 Delcina Drive

River Vale, NJ 07675

Phone: (201) 505–9451

Fax: (201) 573–4094

E-mail: rwbly@bly.com

Web: *www.bly.com*

And now, let's get started, because he who hesitates is lost.

Chapter 1

Work Habits That Speed You Up

"I am always quarreling with time! It is so short to do something and so long to do nothing."
—Queen Charlotte, heir to the British throne (1796–1817)

The ability to work faster and get more done in less time isn't slavery; it's freedom. You're going to have the same big pile of stuff to do every day whether you want it or not. If you can be more efficient, you can get it done and still have some time left over for yourself—whether it's to golf, play with your kids, jog, snowboard, or go fishing.

Make To-Do Lists

Productive workers have schedules and stick with them. But according to an article in *The Competitive Advantage,* more than 50 percent of workers don't schedule their daily activities.

It's not enough to know the projects you're working on. You should break your day into segments. I suggest using hour increments, although quarter and half days can also work. Write down on a piece of paper the project you will work on during each of those segments.

Do this every day, at the beginning of your workday (or, if you prefer, do it the last thing in the day to prepare for the next day). Post your hour-by-hour schedule for the day on a wall or a corkboard by your desk so it is always in view.

Although I may work on a particular project for more than one hour a day, these hours need not be scheduled consecutively. It's up to you.

As you go through the day, consult your schedule to keep on track. If priorities change, you can change the schedule, but do this in writing. Revise and post the schedule. Keeping your schedule on your computer makes this a simple task you can do in minutes.

Why do hour increments work so well? Precisely because they give you a deadline—one hour—to get things done. "Work expands so as to fill time available for its completion," writes C. Northcote Parkinson in his book *Parkinson's Law* (Houghton Mifflin). If you have all day to do task X, you'll take all day. If you have only an hour, you'll work that much more quickly and efficiently.

It's okay to redo the schedule as long as you don't miss deadlines. Some days I redo the daily to-do schedule two or three times, depending on deadlines and inspiration. Why not? As long as you are organized, keep track of deadlines, and allow enough time to finish each job, you will increase your productivity by working on things you feel in the mood to work on.

The 3 To-Do Lists You Should Keep

"Under conditions of complexity, not only are checklists a help, they are required for success," writes Atul Gawande in his book *The Checklist*

Manifesto (Metropolitan Books). "There may be no field or profession where checklists wouldn't be tremendously beneficial."

The key component of my personal productivity system is a series of lists I keep on my computer. In fact, I have so many lists that I have a sub-directory called "Lists" to keep track of them!

That way, I make sure the set of lists I review each day covers every one of my tasks.

Making lists is a simple idea, but extremely effective. Some people credit Ivy Lee, one of the first management consultants, for first using lists as a formal time-management system.

As the story goes, Charles Schwab, president of Bethlehem Steel in the early 1900s, couldn't seem to get enough done. Details and minor matters were crowding the time he urgently needed to consider more important matters. He asked Ivy Lee what to do about it.

Lee handed Schwab a blank sheet of paper. "Write down," he said, "the most important things you have to do tomorrow. The first thing tomorrow morning, start working on item number one, and stay with it until completed. Then take item number two the same way. Then number three, and so on. Don't worry if you don't complete everything on the schedule. At least you will have accomplished the most important projects before getting to the less important ones."

The steel executive tried the idea and recommended it to his associates because the method worked so well. When Schwab asked Lee what his fee was, Lee replied, "Pay me what you think the idea is worth." Schwab reportedly sent Lee a check for $25,000—a fortune in those days (*Time Management: The Art of Getting Things Done.*)

"If you are thinking that lists can be confining, you'll soon learn that once you get used to using them, you'll find them liberating," writes Dan Kennedy in *No B.S. Time Management for Entrepreneurs* (Self Counsel Press). "The more details you get on paper, the fewer you must remember and worry about. This frees your mind up for more important tasks."

Every morning, I come into the office and turn on my computer. After checking my various online services for e-mail, I open the "LISTS" subdirectory; it tells me which lists I must read and review to start my day.

The most important lists on my LISTS directory are my to-do lists. I keep several, but the most critical are my daily to-do list, projects to-do list, and long-term to-do list:

1. **Daily to-do list.** Each day I type up and post a list of the items I have to do that day. From this list, I create my hour-by-hour schedule. This list is revised daily. I enjoy work and put in long hours, so I take on a lot of projects that interest me. But I never take on more than I can handle, so I can continue to meet all deadlines.

2. **Projects to-do list.** In a separate computer file, I keep a list of all of my projects currently under contract, along with the deadline for each. I review this list several times a week, using it to make sure the daily to-do list covers all essential items that have to be done right away.

3. **Long-term to-do list.** This is a list of projects I want to do at some point, but are not now under contract and therefore do not have any assigned deadlines. I check this list about once a week, and usually put in a few hours each week on one of the projects from this list that interests me most. These projects are not urgent (no one is asking me for them) but they are important in that they help me achieve my long-term goals (see Chapter 3).

This simple system works. Most of the techniques throughout this book are simple, yet powerful, so don't be put off by their brevity or ease of implementation. I agree with Texaco CEO Peter Bijur, who said, "As soon as you start to introduce complexity, whether it's into an organization or a set of responsibilities, the more difficult it is to operate." I also agree with Hair Club for Men CEO Sy Sperling: "Simple solutions are the best solutions."

"Lists work only if they are 100-percent leak proof," notes personal productivity coach David Allen in an interview with *Fast Company* magazine. For instance, if your "to-call" list doesn't include all of the phone calls you have to make, then your mind still has to remember some of them.

Determine Priorities

Can you always work on what you want to work on, right when you want to work on it? No. Sometimes, a pressing deadline means putting aside a more pleasurable task to do something more formidable—even if you don't feel like doing it immediately.

On the wall of my office near my desk, I have posted a list that I update every week. It's called "Rules of the Office," and it reminds me of what I have to do to be successful in my business. Rule #1 is "First things first." This means that you must set priorities and meet deadlines.

For instance, if I am burning to work on a book but have a report due the next morning, I write the report first, get it done, and e-mail it to the client. Then I reward myself with an afternoon spent on the book. If I indulged myself and worked on the book first, I'd risk not leaving myself enough time to get my report written by the deadline.

Another "Rule of the Office" worth quoting here is Rule #2: "Make sure it's a working meeting." This rule reminds me to avoid meetings unless there is a set working agenda. A recent survey from NFO Research, reported in *Continental* magazine, shows that the average business professional attends more than 60 meetings a month, and that U.S. employees now spend more than one-third of their time in meetings.

Half of these meetings are unnecessary or inefficient, according to the article. Before agreeing to attend a meeting, find out what topics will be discussed and see if a solution can be reached without a formal meeting. Half of the problems usually can. Ben Stein, actor, novelist, and TV game show host, was once asked how he got so much accomplished. "It's simple," said Stein. "I don't go to meetings."

Meetings can be one of the biggest time-robbers. In *Team Up for Success* (AMI Publishing), Charles Caldwell gives the following tips for managing meeting time:

☺ Decide in advance when meetings will start and stop. Let participants know this information before the meeting begins.

☺ Start and stop on schedule. Start on time even if everyone isn't there.

⊕ Schedule time blocks for each item to be discussed. Make sure meeting participants know how much time is allotted for each item.

⊕ Keep track of time. Comments such as, "We have only 30 minutes left," help keep people on track.

Want to make meetings shorter? Take the chairs out of the room! According to Allen Bluedorn, associate professor of management at the University of Missouri, in an article in *Psychology Today,* meetings in which all participants stand are a third shorter than sit-down conferences—yet the decisions made in them are just as sound.

Overcome Procrastination

"Procrastination," says entrepreneur Victor Kiam, "is opportunity's assassin."

Procrastination is the single biggest factor causing people to fall behind in their work, miss deadlines, and turn in shoddy efforts. P.T. Barnum advised, "Never defer for a single hour that which can be done just as well now." Scientist Thomas Huxley noted, "No good is ever done by hesitation."

Having a daily to-do list—and then assigning yourself various tasks throughout the day in one-hour increments—helps you stay on track and avoid putting things off.

As long as you have your short-term deadlines and long-term goals in mind, you can be somewhat flexible in your daily schedule, adjusting tasks and time slots to match your enthusiasm for each project.

Breaking tasks into one-hour sessions, and then juggling the schedule to work on what interests you most right now, helps overcome procrastination: When you get tired or run out of ideas on one project, just switch to another.

Give yourself rewards for accomplishing tasks. If you work for a solid hour on a budget that's slow going, reward yourself with a break to read your mail or walk around the office building. If you stick with your schedule for the whole morning, treat yourself to your favorite food for lunch.

The best way to make every hour of every day productive is to have an hour-by-hour schedule. People who have such a schedule know what they should be doing every minute and, therefore, do it. People who don't set a schedule tend to drift through the day, stopping and then starting tasks, jumping from job to job, without getting much done.

As Henry Ford observed, "Nothing is particularly hard if you divide it into small jobs." Any project that seems overwhelming can be made less intimidating by breaking it into component parts, phases, or sections—and then working on these parts one at a time. In fact, the whole basis of project management is to break projects into tasks and tasks into activities. Then schedule each and do each small activity by the deadline on the schedule.

In the same way, virtually anyone can handle a series of one-hour jobs during the day with ease. Even four or five one-hour sessions in a day will get things done. Make the list of project steps, post it on your wall, and start step one. In *Scottish Proverbs* (Birlinn Limited), Colin S.K. Walker notes, "Half the battle with work is getting started."

Procrastinators frequently miss deadlines. They complete assignments at the last minute, allowing no time to review the work before handing it in. And they put themselves and their colleagues under undue stress.

Putting off unpleasant, routine, or difficult chores is human nature. Those who discipline themselves to tackle the things they dislike or fear gain self-confidence and make better use of their time.

The following techniques can help you overcome procrastination:

- Imagine how great you'll feel when the chore is completed. Think positively about its outcome.

- If the project is complex or overwhelming, break it down into a series of steps to be entered on your "Things To Do" list. Then set up a specific time and date to begin working on the first step, and follow through as if it were an appointment. Promise to spend 60 minutes a day on the task until it's done, and schedule these daily segments at the same time each day—preferably for a quiet period when there will be no interruptions.

- ⏰ Create an incentive by promising yourself a special reward for getting the job done.

- ⏰ Realize that the task doesn't have to be done perfectly. Some attempt is better than no attempt. Maybe you can do only part of the job and then pass it along to someone else for completion.

- ⏰ Delegate or outsource segments of the work you find boring or distasteful. You can gain precious hours, energy, and enthusiasm by passing along mundane, peripheral, or partly finished work to subordinates or co-workers. The more routine jobs you can delegate, the more time you'll have for other things.

Don't procrastinate another second. Start attacking things now. "Putting off an easy thing makes it hard," observes George Claude Lorimer. "Putting off a hard thing makes it impossible."

Eliminate Bad Habits That Waste Time

First, identify any bad habits you have that waste your time. For me, it was sleeping an hour after I first woke up in the morning. Because the morning is the most productive work time for me, by forcing myself to get dressed and go to the office when I wake up, instead of falling back into bed, I increased my productivity tremendously.

For you, it may be watching a soap opera in the middle of the day, spending too much time surfing the Web, talking in chat rooms or on the phone, doing housework, playing around with apps on your iPhone, or staying up too late at night to read or watch television. Television not only wastes your life but may actually shorten it: According to an article in *The Week,* a new study found that each additional hour spent sitting in front of the TV every day increases the risk of dying by 11 percent.

After you have identified the bad habits, make a list of the ones you must avoid. Phrase each item on your list in the imperative voice. For example, if your worst time-wasting habit is procrastination, this should read as "Don't procrastinate" on your list. If you take on too many ancillary responsibilities because you hate saying no, this item should appear on your list as "Learn to say no."

Post this list in your office in a place where you will always see it, such as on the wall in front of you or on your bulletin board or door. Or place it in a desk drawer where you will see it every day. With this list of bad habits visible, you will be reminded constantly to avoid them and correct behaviors that waste time. Before long, you'll see a big improvement and will be getting more done in less time. Try it!

Avoid Distractions

Outside distractions can be a major time-waster, if you let them. An outside distraction is any unscheduled activity that interrupts the task you are currently working on. For instance, if you're dedicated in the morning to working on a report, and a colleague asks you to call a customer to help resolve an immediate technical problem, that's an outside distraction.

The key is to physically block out disturbances as much as possible, whether by shutting your door, turning your desk away from passersby, letting your voice mail take your calls, posting a "Do Not Disturb" sign, working at home for part of the day, or asking people to be quiet. Your mind can successfully tune out a great many signals if you tell it to.

If interruptions are a real problem, try setting aside a period every day during which you will meet with people and take phone calls. The rest of the time is "private time" during which you can work, uninterrupted. Many people say they accomplish more when they work on a task uninterrupted for as long as they want to.

The main idea is to do things on your schedule, rather than the schedules of others. It's not always possible—but the more you control your time, the more you'll be in control of your life.

Use the 80/20 Rule

The 80/20 rule states that 80 percent of your accomplishments come from only 20 percent of your efforts. The trick is to figure out what makes that 20 percent so productive. Then, devote more of your time to these productive activities, and reduce time spent on unproductive work. To analyze how you spend your time, keep a log of your daily activities for about two weeks.

The next step is to find solutions to these time-wasters. Can you create form letters for replying to correspondence or have your assistant draft replies? Maybe you can create a convenient form that can be used to handle a particular type of communication, eliminating the need to draft a memo every time such an instance arises. Could you or an assistant clean up and organize the filing system? How about combining business trips, or scheduling travel time for off hours? For instance, scheduling an out-of-town meeting for Monday morning permits you to fly out Sunday evening, so you don't lose part of a workday in travel.

Make and Use Standard Operating Procedures

Manufacturing mass-produced items is profitable and efficient because it's so cookie-cutter: Each widget is exactly like the one before it. That being the case, the steps in manufacturing all the widgets on the assembly line are the same. Therefore, these steps can be documented in writing, making them simple and easy to follow.

White-collar professionals can benefit from this essentially blue-collar productivity booster: Instead of reinventing the wheel each time, do what you did the last time you faced a similar situation. Or do something similar. Learn from repetition. Isolate the steps. Save components and parts (images, text, spreadsheets) you can reuse. Be as efficient as the factory line making widgets. Break each task into tiny steps. Write them down as a standard operating procedure. Refer to this document whenever you have to do the task. In my office, we get a lot of inquiries about my services, and we have developed a written procedure for handling them, ensuring that no steps are omitted.

Take customer service, for instance. Many customer service departments waste an enormous amount of time answering questions, especially from new customers, that they've answered over and over again. My friend David Yale has a neat solution: First, survey your customer-service staff to find out the most common questions they get from new customers. Then answer these questions in a "welcome kit" that you send to all new customers. Your customer service burden should decrease, says Yale. The cost of the kit? Less than a dollar.

What else do you do that's routine and could be turned into a standard operating procedure? Get computer software and other tools to help you automate these processes. Don't engage in time-consuming problem-solving when there's a recipe that could be followed more easily and more productively. If you had to make a pie, for instance, why would you perform chemical analysis of other pies to determine the compounds in the crust when you could just look it up in a cookbook? Yet people do the equivalent every day. What a waste!

You need not invent or document these procedures yourself, if you don't want to. There are a ton of them available from a variety of sources, yours for the asking. If you don't know how to do something—clean a fax machine, change your oil, fire an employee—go to the library, the bookstore, or the World Wide Web. Chances are the complete directions are already there, waiting for you to read and learn from them.

Adjust Your Schedule to Your Energy Levels

Most of us have certain times during the day when we're most alert and perform better. Once you've determined your pattern of physical and mental energy levels, try to adjust your daily schedule to mesh with it. By handling mentally demanding jobs during your peak energy periods, you can get more done in less time. Fit your schedule to your moods and energy levels, and you'll find that you'll save time and be more effective in your job.

Most of us cannot control the hours we favor. Dr. Nathaniel Kleitman, a physiologist at the University of Chicago, says body temperature varies by up to three degrees during each day. When your body temperature drops, you have maximum energy. When it rises, your energy wanes. (This may explain why, according to a recent survey, most people say they would rather be too cold than too hot.)

Dr. Emmanuel Mignot, co-author of a study published in the journal *Sleep* (and published in *The Record*), says his research team may have found variations in a particular gene that determine whether you prefer to rise early or stay up late. Although further research is needed to confirm the finding, Mignot suggests that if it's true, work schedules in the future may be arranged so people handle the toughest tasks during periods when they are most likely to be productive.

So if you are a night owl, burning the midnight oil may result in maximum productivity for you. If you are an early bird, get up early and start working while everyone else in your house is still asleep.

Other people find that they can alter their circadian rhythm deliberately by changing when they go to bed and get up. If you have a choice of whether to be an early-morning person or a late-nighter, and your schedule allows you to do either, pick the one that works best for you.

If all else is equal, choose the morning. When you start early in the morning, as I do, you have the benefit of having completed a significant amount of your day's work quota by the time others are first stumbling into their offices. Early starters finish the day's work early and have the rest of the time to do more work or play. Late starters are behind from the moment they get up and feel increasing pressure to get their work done as the hour grows even later.

The easiest productivity tip in the world is to get up and start working an hour earlier than you normally do. Freelance writer Charles Flowers says whenever he has a deadline or a lot of work on a given day, he gets up as early as he must to meet that deadline, even if it means rising at 5 in the morning. I have, on some days, been at the office as early as 3 or 4 a.m., although this is rare.

Maintain Peak Energy During the Day

Energy is a function of many factors, one of them being enthusiasm. When you are enthusiastic, your energy can remain high, even if you are physically tired. When you are bored, your energy drains, and you become lethargic and unproductive.

To maintain peak productivity and energy, maintain peak enthusiasm and avoid boredom. The main cause of boredom is not doing what you want, when you want to do it. Therefore, you should structure your work so you are spending most of your time doing what you want, when you feel like doing it.

Obviously, you should shy away from assignments that bore you, when you can. Forcing yourself to work on things you dislike will drain your energy. Even those assignments that interest you can get boring if you work on them for too long or if you don't feel like doing them at the time. The solution is to have many different projects and to work on the ones you want to work on at any given time. Because you largely set your own hourly schedule each day (meetings are an exception), you can do tasks in the order that pleases you, as long as you meet your deadlines.

Of course, when a deadline is looming, you may have no choice but to put aside work you want to do and focus on what has to be done to meet that deadline. Even this is avoidable if you negotiate sufficient deadlines and then plan your time so you get started early, rather than waiting until the last minute as so many people do.

Everyone finds something that can help revitalize them throughout the day. When you find what works for you, do it. My office has a private bathroom, and when I feel my concentration and energy waning, I wash my hair. I become immediately refreshed—perhaps the wet head of hair cools my overheated brain. You can take a break and re-energize by washing your face, taking a walk, running errands, meeting a friend for coffee, or chatting on the phone.

Design a Productive Workspace

A computer tech I recently hired to do some work for me commented, "I really like your computer system. Everything is in easy reach." He then mentioned that in many personal computer systems, the owners put vital components, such as the CPU or disk drive or printer, on the floor, under a desk, or otherwise out of reach. I've seen that, and I feel that it wastes effort and time. My philosophy is that everything you need—computer systems, office equipment, the telephone, supplies, reference materials, files—should be reachable just by swiveling your chair and reaching out to the appropriate cabinet, shelf, or drawer—without having to get out of your seat.

Plenty of desk space and file cabinet storage also boost productivity. All the materials I need—files, reference books, supplies, computer equipment, telephone, fax, copier—are right at hand. I can swivel in my chair or reach over to get what I need, without getting up and trekking across the room.

Make sure you have adequate space to organize and store work materials so they're close at hand and easy to find. Having to search for a book or folder wastes time and can cause you to lose your pace when you're in a productive groove. Get an L-shaped desk that gives you double the surface area of a standard desk.

When you build your reference library, be generous, yet selective. This means don't acquire a book, CD ROM, or other reference material unless it relates to the subjects you work on. By the same token, if you see a book you know would be useful, buy it right then and there. Don't hesitate because of the price. It's a small investment to save valuable time later on getting information you need.

10 Tips to Help You Work Better and Faster

1. **Use a computer.** Anyone in any business who wants to be productive (from the manager of an insurance company to a contractor scheduling appointments) should use a modern PC with the latest software. Doing so can double, triple, or even quadruple your output. (Chapter 7 guides you on the technology you should acquire and how to use it.)

2. **Don't be a perfectionist.** "I'm a non-perfectionist," said Isaac Asimov, author of 475 books. "I don't look back in regret or worry at what I have written." Be a careful worker, but don't agonize over your work beyond the point where the extra effort no longer produces a proportionately worthwhile improvement in your final product.

   Be excellent but not perfect. Customers do not have the time or budget for perfection; for most projects, getting 95 to 98 percent of the way to perfection is good enough. That doesn't mean you deliberately make errors or give less than your best. It means you stop polishing and fiddling with the job when it looks good to you—and you don't agonize over the fact that you're not spending another hundred hours on it. Create it, check it, and then let it go.

   Understand the exponential curve of excellence. Quality improves with effort according to an exponential curve. That means that early effort yields the biggest results; subsequent efforts yield smaller and smaller improvements, until eventually the miniscule return is not worth the effort. Productive people stop at the point where the investment in further effort on a task is no longer justified by the tiny incremental improvement it would produce. Aim for 100-percent perfection and you are unlikely to be productive or profitable. Consistently hit within the 90- to 98-percent range and you will maximize both customer satisfaction as well as return on your time investment.

"Perfection does not exist," wrote Alfred de Musset. "To understand this is the triumph of human intelligence; to expect to possess it is the most dangerous kind of madness."

3. **Free yourself from the pressure to be an innovator.** As publisher Cameron Foote observes, "Clients are looking for good, not great." Do your best to meet the client's or your boss's requirements. They will be happy. Do not feel pressured to reinvent the wheel or create a masterpiece on every project you take on. Don't be held up by the false notion that you must uncover some great truth or present your boss with revolutionary ideas and concepts. Most successful business solutions are just common sense packaged to meet a specific need.

Eliminate performance anxiety. Don't worry about whether what you are doing is different or better than what others have done before you. Just do the best you can. That will be enough.

4. **Switch back and forth between different tasks.** Even if you consider yourself a specialist, do projects outside your specialty. Inject variety into your schedule. Arrange your daily schedule so you switch off from one assignment to another at least once or twice each day. Variety, as the saying goes, is indeed the spice of life.

Approximately 70 to 90 percent of what I am doing at any time is in tasks within my area of expertise. This keeps me highly productive. The other 10 to 30 percent is in new areas, markets, industries, or disciplines outside my area of expertise. This keeps me fresh and allows me to explore things that captivate my imagination but are not in my usual schedule of assignments.

5. **Don't waste time working on projects you don't have yet.** Get letters of agreement, contracts, purchase orders, and budget sign-offs before proceeding. Don't waste time starting the work for projects

that may not come to fruition. An official approval or go-ahead from your boss or from a customer makes the project real, so you can proceed at full speed with the confidence and enthusiasm that come from knowing you have been given the green light.

6. **Make deadlines firm but adequate.** According to *Continental* magazine, of 150 executives surveyed by AccounTemps, 37 percent rated the dependable meeting of deadlines as the most important quality of a team player.

Productive people set and meet deadlines. Without a deadline, the motivation to do a task is small to nonexistent. Tasks without assigned deadlines automatically go to the bottom of your priority list. After all, if you have two reports to file—where one is due a week from Thursday, and the other due "whenever you can get around to it"—which do you suppose will get written first?

Often you will collaborate with your supervisor or customer in determining deadlines. Set deadlines for a specific date and time, not a time period (for example, "due November 23rd by 3 p.m. or sooner," not "in about two weeks"). Having a specific date and time for completion eliminates confusion and gives you motivation to get the work done on time.

At the same time, don't make deadlines too tight. Try to build in a few extra days for the unexpected, such as a missing piece of information, a delay from a subcontractor, a last-minute change, or a crisis on another project.

7. **Protect and value your time.** Productive people guard their time more heavily than the gold in Fort Knox. They don't waste time. They get right to the point. They may come off as abrupt or dismissive to some people. But they realize they cannot give everyone who contacts them all the time each person wants. They determine how much time to spend with each person. They make decisions. They say what needs to be said, do what needs to be done, and then move on.

Respect hour power. One successful entrepreneur told me he doesn't wear a watch and never knows what time it is. He's the exception, not the rule. Most busy and successful people I've met are aware of the relentless pressure of time. They keep track of it like they would watch a limited inventory of a precious raw material in a manufacturing plant.

If you watch successful, experienced poker players, they will carefully divide money into piles of coins and bills, sorted by denomination. Successful time managers divide their days into hourly increments in much the same way—and spend them even more carefully.

Think of your time this way: Assign a dollar value to each hour. Whether staff or independent, salaried or hourly, every productive person can tell you the worth of his or her time. Let's say you mow lawns for a living and can do two lawns per hour. If your fee is $15 per lawn, the hour value of your time is $30. Productive people weigh the effort required for specific activities—and the return it will produce—against the cost of the time based on the dollar value of their hour. Maybe the lawn professional wants to add hedge-clipping as a service. If he can charge $20 per hedge and do four in an hour, that's an $80-per-hour return. Based on his current hourly worth of $30, it's an extremely profitable move.

8. **Stay focused.** As Robert Ringer, best-selling author of *Looking Out For #1,* observes, successful people apply themselves to the task at hand. They work until the work gets done.

They concentrate on one or two things at a time. They don't go in a hundred different directions. My experience is that people who are big talkers—constantly spouting ideas or proposing deals and ventures—are spread out in too many different directions to be effective. Efficient people have a vision, and they focus their activities to achieve that vision.

To focus on what you do best, make only what you add value to—and buy the rest around the corner. Wolverine, a member of the X-Men team of comic book super heroes, frequently comments, "I'm the best there is at what I do." (In his case, it's beating bad guys.) Productive workers spend their time doing what they do better and faster than anyone else. To gain more of these profitable hours, they outsource and delegate other tasks to vendors and subordinates. There are endless ways to spend your time, if you want to pursue them all. Unfortunately, your time is anything but endless. Productivity means selectivity. Don't attempt to do everything. You can't even come close, so why bother?

9. **Set a production goal.** Stephen King writes 1,500 words every day except on his birthday, Christmas, and the Fourth of July. Steinway makes 800 pianos in its German plant every year.

   Workers and organizations that want to meet deadlines and be successful set a production goal and achieve it. An individual who truly wants to be productive sets a production goal, meets it, and then keeps going until he or she can do no more—or runs out of time—for the day.

   Joe Lansdale, author of *Bad Chili* (Mysterious Press) and many other novels, says he never misses his productivity goal of writing three pages a day, five days a week. "I'm not in the mood; I don't feel like it; what kind of an excuse is that?" Lansdale said in an interview with *Publishers Weekly*. "If I'm not in the mood, do I not go to the chicken plant if I've got a job in the chicken plant?"

10. **Do work you enjoy.** In advising people on choosing their life's work, David Ogilvy, founder of the advertising agency Ogilvy & Mather, quotes a Scottish proverb that says, "Be happy while you're living; for you're a long time dead." The Tao Te Ching says, "In work, do what you enjoy."

    When you enjoy your work, it really isn't work. To me, success is being able to make a good living while spending the workday in pleasurable tasks. You won't love every project equally, of course, but try to balance "must-do" mandatory tasks with things that are more fun for you. Seek assignments that are exciting, interesting, and fulfilling.

In addition to enjoying their work, many super-productive people gain enjoyment from the act of being super-productive itself. These people aren't necessarily workaholics. They are proud of their accomplishments—and their efficiency. My definition of a productive, efficient person is someone who can do in a day what others take a week to accomplish.

Talk to super-productive people. Many get a rush out of being super-efficient time managers, in addition to the pleasure they derive from simply being competent in their job, profession, or skill set. I love doing good work. But I also get a thrill out of doing two projects in a week when my colleagues are only doing one.

Can you train yourself to like work better and enjoy it more? Motivational experts say we have the ability to change our attitudes and behavior. "Attitude is a trap or it is freedom. Create your own," writes Judy Crookes in *Inner Realm* magazine.

Whatever your motivation, use it to enjoy not only having a good job, but doing the work itself. My motivation is avoiding boredom. Every day that I come into my office and turn on the computer, I'm thankful that I can make a good living writing, and therefore don't have to do some other job that would bore me.

Many professionals in all fields love their work so much, they never stop. English major Lee Falk, for example, created The Phantom, which was recently made into a feature film, in 1936. Six decades later, Falk, in his 80s, was still writing the comic strip, which appears daily.

"Enjoy your achievements as well as your plans," advised Max Ehrmann in his 1927 essay "Desiderata." "Keep interested in your own career, however humble; it is a real possession in the changing fortunes of time."

Mark Gruenwald, a senior editor at Marvel Comics, loved his work so much that when he died in 1996, he left a request that his ashes be mixed into the ink used to reprint a superhero series he had written. According to an article in the *Daily News* (August 29, 1997), his wish was granted. "He has truly become one with the story," said his widow, Catherine Gruenwald.

One other point: Achieving a noticeable increase in personal productivity needn't be a quantum leap or radical change. Just adapt two or three of the suggestions in this chapter. Practice them on a daily basis. In no time, you will begin to see light at the end of the tunnel of busyness—and the picture will only get brighter from there.

Chapter 2

Do You Really Want to Be Productive?

"Time is a precious possession and I attempt to make the most of it by not wasting it, for it is irreplaceable."
—Stanley Marcus, *Minding the Store* (University of N. Texas Press)

If you want to be super-productive, there are certain things you will have to give up. These things include the extravagant luxuries of sloth, inertia, laziness, and wasted idle time. If you are not willing to give these up, you must seriously question whether being more productive is truly a priority in your life. If it isn't, that's okay. However, don't complain that there's "never enough time," and then watch 25 hours of sports on TV each weekend.

The primary reason most workers are not productive is that they do not really desire it. Isaac Asimov wanted to write a lot of books, so he designed his life to increase his output. (This included focusing on topics on which he could produce books quickly and avoiding travel, so he could spend most of his time in his study.) This chapter presents guidelines to help you assess whether being productive is important to you, and whether you are willing to do what is necessary to achieve superior productivity.

Set Your Goals High

Many workers who are ambitious look at other workers, see what they produce, and set their own goals slightly higher.

Unfortunately, this won't make you productive. The majority of workers have limited outputs. So even if you do a little more than they do, your output will still be small.

Do not use the average worker as a role model for productivity. Most people do not set their sights high enough. For instance, upon hearing that a famous novelist was coming out with his first new novel in half a decade, Stephen King once commented, "Come on...it doesn't take five years to write a novel."

We productive workers want to get the job done, polish it, and move on to the next task. We care about quality, but we strive for excellence rather than perfection.

I've found that productive professionals admire other productive people precisely because these workers are productive. In his autobiography, *It Came From Ohio!* (Scholastic Books), R.L. Stine, author of 250 books, comments, "I read an article about a writer in South America who has written over a thousand books! Sometimes he writes three books a day! My hero!"

Stine, incidentally, says he works six or seven days a week to write two books every month. The late Isaac Asimov worked seven days a week from 7:30 a.m. to 10:30 p.m., stopping only for business lunches, social engagements, telephone conversations, and other activities he referred to as "interruptions."

Although you don't have to be a workaholic to be a productive worker, it does help. Most workers who are more productive than their peers work more than just from 9 to 5. Claude Hopkins, one of the most successful advertising executives of all time, said he got twice as much accomplished as everyone else in his agency because he worked twice as hard and twice as long.

Thomas Edison, the productive inventor, bragged about being a workaholic who only slept four or five hours a night. Frank Reich, the inventor of Tufoil motor oil additive, told me that, while he was in the throes of pursuing his invention, he moved a cot into his lab so he could sleep there and not waste time going back and forth between his lab and his house.

I am not telling you to be a workaholic or sacrifice the rest of your life. But in a sense, to be productive at anything, some sacrifices must be made. Entrepreneur Andrew Linick points out that everything we want—everything we want to do, learn, achieve, or create—has a price. That price is time. Productive workers pay this price to be productive. If you're not willing to pay it, there's a limit to what you can do.

Set realistic, but ambitious, goals. Do not be afraid to take on challenges and try new things. "In order to succeed at almost anything, it's necessary to risk failure at various times along the way," advises Dr. Joyce Brothers in her newspaper column (in *New York Daily News*).

"If you stay committed, your dreams can come true," says Michael Blake, who wrote the movie *Dances With Wolves.* "I left home at 17 and had nothing but rejections for 25 years. I wrote more than 20 screenplays, but I never gave up."

Enjoy Your Work

The majority of Americans really dislike their work. "Everybody but a complete idiot or a college professor who has never had a lick of work in their lives looks forward to quitting time, and the sooner it comes the better," a factory worker told Benjamin Hunnicutt, author of *Kellogg's Six-Hour Day* (Temple University Press). But as Marilyn Machlowitz observes in *Workaholics* (New American Library), "When work is a joy and not just a job, it is never odious or arduous."

Learn to like the work you do. If you find something you enjoy and are good at, you will not be able to stop long enough to get a good night's sleep. Here's more evidence that the more you love your work, the more energized and productive you can be.

- Psychologist Mihaly Csikszentmihalyi has coined the term *flow,* in *Flow* (HarperCollins), to describe the state of mind people are in when they love their work. According to this theory, flow is a state in which people are so involved in an activity that nothing else seems to matter; the experience is so enjoyable that people will do it even at great cost. If you've ever been so wrapped up in what you were doing that you didn't want to stop, you were probably in flow. The more you are in flow, the more you will enjoy work, and the more productive you will be.

- Naturalist Sigurd Olson comments, "Give me work which I like to do." The question he asks himself to determine whether he can be productive in a job is: "Can I lose myself in this work, wrap my entire being up in it...or will it be just another job again?" (Quoted in *A Wilderness Within: The Life of Sigurd F. Olson* by David Backes; University of Minnesota Press.)

- Herb Kelleher, CEO of Southwest Airlines, was cited in *Computerwold* as saying: "I work most of the time. I enjoy what I do. My vocation is my avocation. If you enjoy what you do there's no stress connected to it. Every day is a pleasure."

- Winston Churchill once said, "Those whose work and pleasures are one are fortune's favorite children."

Value Your Time

Almost everyone complains about not having enough time. Yet the way many people act shows they place almost no value on their time. That's contradictory and a shame.

Everyone's time has value. To understand this value and make it meaningful, you need to assign an actual dollar-per-hour value to your time.

Then, when you make decisions about how to spend your time, you weigh the hourly cost against the potential reward from the activity you're considering. If it doesn't pay off, don't do it.

For instance, my wife has a friend, Mary, who spends a lot of her time driving to different stores to hunt down the best sales. She proudly boasts about saving $1 on paper towels or getting a product that costs $25 at the nearby mall for only $16 at a discount outlet 15 miles away.

To Mary, this represents real savings and a source of pride. To me, it's a waste of time. When you factor in time spent, gas, tolls, and the wear and tear on Mary's car, the so-called bargain is no bargain at all. To me, that's too high a price to pay to "save" a few dollars. Mary sees money in absolute terms; she doesn't factor in the value of her time.

How do you assign a dollar value to your time? If you are self-employed and charge by the hour for your services, the worth of your time is readily apparent. Likewise, hourly employees have a clear picture of the worth of their time: If they earn $14.88 an hour, wasting an hour costs $14.88.

My lawyer, for example, charges $200 an hour. Instead of taking an hour to go to a discount mall and save $9, he could spend the hour doing billable work and make $200. Even if he misses out on the discount savings, he comes out $191 ahead for the hour.

Even if you don't charge or get paid by the hour, your time still has a dollar value. Calculating it is easy. If you are paid $50,000 a year, your time is worth about $1,000 a week. If you put in a 40-hour week, that comes to $25 per hour. When you are tempted to do a nonessential activity, keep that $25-per-hour figure in mind. That's what it costs to waste an hour.

Take coupons, for example. People I know can't understand why I don't use coupons when buying groceries at the supermarket. "You're paying too much!" they exclaim. "You could get it cheaper!" They don't understand that it's not just money that has a value; time does, too. When I calculate the time and energy required to look for, clip, save, file, and retrieve coupons, search for products, and remember to use coupons, it's not worth it to me.

Last week in the supermarket, I was picking up a package of butter when a man tapped me on the shoulder. "Don't buy that now," he advised me in a friendly tone. "Come back tomorrow. It will be on sale—one dollar off."

I smiled and thanked him for the information—and bought the butter. To go back to the store the following day, rather than buy the butter on the spot, would take at least 20 minutes. Is my time or yours truly worth only $3 an hour? That's apparently what my butter-bargain-hunting friend believes. I don't.

My wife, Amy, doesn't always agree with this idea of weighing the dollar value of time against the dollar savings or costs of the alternatives. One morning, when my car was at the repair station for service, she objected to my plan to call a taxi to take me to work. "Relax," I said. "My office is only two miles away and the ride costs about $6."

"Why waste $6?" she replied. "I have the mini-van. I'll drop you off when I take the kids to school."

"That won't get me to the office until 8:45," I objected. "The taxi will get me there by 7:30. If I wait for you, I'll lose over an hour of productive work time."

She fumed and protested, but I took a cab anyway. At the time, my billing rate for my consulting service was a couple of hundred dollars an hour. Yet Amy saw the $6 cab ride as a waste of money. Two different mind-sets. If you want to be super-productive, follow mine.

Here are some suggestions for making the most profitable use of your time:

1. Work on critical tasks when you are freshest and most energetic. For me, this is the earlier part of the day—from 7 a.m. until about 1 p.m.

2. If you are very busy this week, don't even leaf through the journals and magazines that come across your desk. Instead, throw them out.

3. Tell people who make social calls that you are too busy to talk and that you will call them back when you're free.

4. When you get tired of working on a project, don't force yourself to continue (unless you're under deadline). Instead, put it aside and work on something else.

5. Try to conduct your activities from your office rather than making trips. Travel can be an enormous time-waster. Travel as much as you have to, but no more. If a transaction can be handled just as effectively via phone, fax, or e-mail, do it that way.

6. Try to eliminate unproductive activities that may be fun but don't lighten your workload. Years ago I gave up college teaching because it was taking away too much time. Be wary of taking on volunteer work just because someone asks you to.

7. Try getting up earlier and putting in an extra hour every morning from Monday through Friday. That's five extra hours of productive time a week.

8. If you are going to work on the weekend, early Saturday morning is a good time. You can get in an extra three to five hours and still have the rest of the weekend free.

Know the Value of Time and Money

Do you need money? Most of us do. Unless you are independently wealthy or have a second source of income, most workers need to earn a paycheck to pay rent or mortgage, health insurance premiums, utility bills, grocery and doctor bills, and for DVD rentals.

My father once told me, "Money is not important, as long as you're happy." I disagree. I share the view of consultant Ted Nicholas. Writing in his Direct Marketing Success Letter, Ted says, "The happiest possible life ideally rests on a balance between four elements: health, career, personal relationships, and money."

Unfortunately, most workers don't have as much personal wealth as they desire. Why is it that so many Americans, even those with executive positions, have such a relatively low net worth? Because they spend too much. Americans are notoriously behind the rest of the world when it comes to accruing wealth. According to the blog econ265 (*econ365.files.wordpress. com/2008/10/gross-savings-rate.pdf*), the average American family saves less than 5 percent of its earnings each year, compared with nearly 10 percent in the UK and almost 13 percent in Sweden.

Productive workers who I have met tend to be partially money-driven or at least money-conscious. They are not content with the meager income of the average worker. They may not all aspire to great wealth, but they all want to be comfortable. My definition of success is this: doing what you want, when and where you want to do it, and getting paid well for it—sometimes very, very well. This is what you can achieve when you are productive and put your nose to the grindstone, your back into your hammer swings, or your fingertips to the computer keys.

A wise person once remarked, "If you don't know where you are going, you are certainly never going to get there." Think about where you're going. How much money do you want? If you answer "enough" or "a lot," you haven't clearly defined your income goals (see Chapter 3). Without knowing where you are going, how will you get there? An important first step toward increasing your income is to set a specific dollar goal.

The purpose of setting this goal is not necessarily to meet it but to provide a target upon which all your efforts can be focused. Even if you do not earn the specific dollar figure, just having a goal and working toward it can increase your earnings far beyond what you would make just aimlessly plodding along. A goal gives you something to set your sights on, inspires hard work, and is a catalyst for success.

Leo Burnett, founder of the advertising agency that created the "Marlboro Man," is credited with the following observation: "If you reach for the stars and fall, you will get the moon. But if you reach just for a tree branch and fall, you will end up in the mud." In other words, it's always better to set your goals a little higher—a little beyond your reach—rather than make them too easy. The goal should be difficult, because success requires hard work and a bit of ambition. If you set easy goals, you will always achieve them, but you'll always achieve below your potential as well.

Another story illustrates this point: Two salespeople decide at the beginning of the year that they will set sales goals. Each writes his goal on a sheet of paper. At the end of the year, they meet. The first salesman opens his paper and says to the second, "See, here is my goal: $50,000 in sales commissions. And I have done it. I achieved my goal!" He turns to his friend. "And how did you do?"

"Not as well," confesses the second salesman. "I set my goal at $1 million in sales commissions—and I, unlike you, have achieved only half of my goal."

You get the point.

Self-Assessment Test: Are You a Productive Worker?

Respond to these statements honestly. Then score yourself and check your rating.

1. I am a perfectionist. I redo work many times, because everything I do must be perfect. ❏ True ❏ False

2. I consider my finished work as a product unto itself, not an ends to satisfy a customer or supervisor. ❏ True ❏ False

3. It's very important to me to be well paid and successful at work. ❏ True ❏ False

4. I would sometimes rather be at the office working than at home doing household chores or leisure activities. ❏ True ❏ False

5. I would be bored at work if I had too little to do. ❏ True ❏ False

6. Being busy and productive is important to my ego and self-esteem. ❏ True ❏ False

7. I find myself constantly keeping track of my productivity, output, and accomplishments. ❏ True ❏ False

8. The fact that I am so productive is the thing people tend to notice most about me, and I like that very much. ❏ True ❏ False

9. My ego is tied to my work. When I have too few projects to do or am waiting to find out whether a big project is going to get the go-ahead from management, I get antsy. ❏ True ❏ False

---

Scoring: For questions 1 and 2, give yourself one point for every false answer and zero points for every true answer. For questions 3 through 9, give yourself one point for every true answer and zero points for every false answer. The more points you have, the closer your personality, attitude, and beliefs are to those of most workers who are productive.

If, after answering these questions, you feel you have the personality of a high-productivity worker, don't fight it. The only way you are going to be really happy is if you are busy and productive. This book shows how to increase your output as well as your income.

On the other hand, if, after taking the test, you feel you don't fit the profile of the productive worker, stop and ask yourself, "Is being productive really important to me? Is making a lot of money really important to me?" If the answer is no, maybe you'd be happier slowing down, being less frantic, and doing your work at a more leisurely pace. But if the answer is yes, how are you going to reconcile your desire to be productive with the fact that you don't share the same attitudes toward work as productive workers? You will either have to change some of your attitudes or habits, or strike a balance between the desire to be productive and successful at work and the desire to spend more of your time at home relaxing.

Avoid Job Burnout

If you decide to pursue greater productivity, be aware of the possibility of burnout. Although being a productive worker can be fulfilling, as human beings we have limits to our energy. If you work too hard, for too long without a break, you can become tired, fall out of "flow," and feel bored, de-energized, even depressed.

You can't always tell when job burnout strikes. In many instances people who feel unhappy or depressed are not able to pinpoint the reason. But job burnout victims often share many of the following feelings and circumstances:

⊕ **Bored.** Every now and then we all have a day when we'd rather be strolling in the park than be stuck in the office. That's only natural. People experiencing job burnout are bored almost all the time. They are turned off by their assignments and have little enthusiasm for the job.

    Job burnout is a stressful situation. It's no fun having to wake up each morning knowing you have to go to a job you despise. The symptoms of stress are different for different people, but be alert to symptoms like nervousness, fatigue, sleeplessness, heartburn, headaches, stomach aches, and constipation. They may be a sign that you are suffering stress caused by job burnout.

- **Overworked.** Do you work too hard? Do you feel pressured by time? By deadlines? Do you say things like "I wish there were 26 hours in the day"? If so, watch out! Overworked people are likely to suffer fatigue and stress that can eventually lead to job burnout.

- **Underworked.** Surprisingly, being underworked is even more likely to lead to burnout than being overworked. The fact is, most people want to work and feel as if they're contributing something to the company. If you're not working at your full potential, you'll feel unproductive and unsatisfied.

One woman recently hired by a government agency complained to me, "I beg for more projects at work, but the supervisors just won't give them to me. I feel like I'm wasting my time. What's the point of being at work eight hours a day if I can complete my assignments by 10:30 in the morning?"

After only six months on the job, this woman is already sending out resumes and looking for a new position. She hopes to land a job with private industry where, she feels, her talents will be put to better use—and she'll avoid job burnout.

- **Time-conscious.** Do you find yourself glancing at your watch more than four times an hour? Have you ever thought that an hour had gone by, but when you looked at your watch, it had been only five minutes? Does the secondhand on the clock seem to move too slowly these days?

Job burnout victims are often extremely time conscious, but in a negative sense. They use the progression of time to help get them through the day, rather than to make the day more productive. And, they find that time on the job passes much more slowly than time at home. People who enjoy their work, on the other hand, find that the business day passes quickly.

- **Difficulty concentrating.** When you enjoy what you're doing, it's easy to tackle the work with enthusiasm and vigor. Job burnout victims have a hard time applying themselves to their work because they find it boring and unfulfilling. If you find yourself staring at the same piece of paper for hours, or reading the same paragraph over and over, or constantly feeling drained and drowsy during the day, you may be a prime candidate for burnout.

🕐 **Low self-esteem.** According to the American work ethic, you are what you do. So if you don't think much of what you do, you won't think much of yourself.

Job burnout victims can get caught in a vicious cycle of self-degradation. Because they're dissatisfied with their job, they think work is a waste of time. Then they feel worthless because they think they're failures in their careers. Making this situation even worse is the fact that some people have an uncanny knack for sensing when others are feeling low and take advantage. This makes those at their lowest point resent themselves and their jobs even more.

🕐 **Withdrawn.** As self-esteem sinks lower and lower, burnout victims become overly introverted and withdrawn. They don't socialize or communicate with coworkers because of their work-inflicted inferiority complex. They look at co-workers who are seemingly satisfied with their jobs and say to themselves, "These people are doing okay. So it must be me, not the company or the job."

🕐 **Can't face the day.** A close friend of mine found he was spending every business morning hanging over the toilet throwing up. The thought of going to work was that distasteful to him. If getting out of bed to face the workday is an agonizing struggle, you probably have an advanced case of job burnout.

Okay. Let's say you think you're suffering from job burnout—either a mild or a severe case. What do you do about it? Here are 10 ways to avoid and overcome job burnout.

1. **Ask for more work.** Not getting a chance to work to your full potential is one of the biggest reasons for job burnout.

   Why don't managers delegate more to their staffs? One reason is that they never learned how: Most managers are doers, not delegators. Another reason is that a poor manager makes him- or herself feel more important by hogging all the work and leaving staffers in the dark.

Working under a manager who refuses to delegate makes people feel frustrated and useless. If you're not being used to your fullest potential, ask for more work. Tell your supervisor that you can tackle more—and that you want more to tackle.

"But I'm not sure you can handle more," your manager may reply.

"Fine," you say. "I'll prove I can." Tell your manager to increase your workload just a little bit at first. Once he or she sees how efficiently and quickly you complete the assignment, you'll be given as much as you can handle.

Unfortunately, some managers are never going to delegate. If you're stuck working for one of them, changing jobs may be your only way out.

2. **Take on different work.** People joke about being stuck in a rut. But it's no joke. One business executive I know defines a rut as "a grave without a cover." Life shouldn't be a grind. It should be enjoyable, fun, even thrilling.

If you feel stuck in a rut, get out. Break your daily routine by doing something new. For example, if you've always wanted to write but never tried it, volunteer to write an article for your company newsletter or a trade journal. If you've always thought sales would be fun but never tried it, volunteer to staff the booth at your company's next trade show exhibit. If you're interested in computers but haven't had much chance to work with them, sign up for your company's in-plant course in Unix or Excel.

3. **Learn something new.** Some people spend their professional lives rehashing and reworking the same limited bits of knowledge they picked up in school and their early training. For instance, an advertising writer I know complained to me that because he had become a specialist in automobiles, he had essentially written and rewritten the same set of ads for a dozen different clients over the course of his 25-year career.

Of course, he could have broken out of this at any time. He could have studied a new area to write about, such as consumer electronics, or soap, or medical products. But he didn't, and the longer he stayed within the narrow confines of automotive copywriting, the harder it became for him to try anything new.

Life and work become dull when you stop learning. So don't. Make it a point to broaden your knowledge, master new skills, and learn new things. For example, instead of throwing away college catalogs and course solicitations you receive in the mail, sign up for a course in a new topic that interests you. Or, if you don't have time for night school, you can always read a book or attend a lecture.

Rehashing the same database of knowledge you've always carried around in your brain is safe and easy. It's also boring and can lead to job burnout. When you're continually learning new things about your work, you keep the interest and excitement level high.

4. **Do something new.** Go on a cruise. Learn to play the clarinet. Build a cedar closet. This new thing that you try doesn't have to be work-related. The simple act of doing something you've never done before will boost your spirits and give you a new outlook on life—a positive attitude that will spill over onto your job.

By continually trying new things, you become well-rounded, and well-rounded people are the most content personally and professionally.

5. **Become more active in your own field.** Somewhere along the way, you may have lost the zest for engineering, science, sales, retail, or business that you had when you first started. The daily grind of 9-to-5 has worn you down. You've forgotten why you became an engineer, a photographer, or whatever it is you do, in the first place.

You can escape job burnout by rekindling your interest in your profession. Join your professional society, if you haven't already. Become active: Attend meetings, read journals, present papers. You can even run for office in your local chapter. Take a course or teach one. Take responsibility for training one of the new employees in your department. The people who are active in their field are usually the most successful and the most satisfied with their careers.

6. **Restructure your job.** An assistant at an advertising agency explained to me the source of her career blues: "I took [an assistant-level] job to get my 'foot in the door' in the advertising business. Although this is my first job in advertising, I have a pretty extensive writing background, mainly in employee communications for several large firms.

"I thought that in an ad agency I'd get an opportunity to put my writing skills to use. But it has not worked out that way. I know I could write very good copy, if I was given a chance. But my boss thinks of me strictly as a secretary, and he has never given me the opportunity to use my talent to write an ad or a commercial."

Perhaps you too have been forced into a role against your will. Maybe you had hopes of doing "creative" projects but found yourself handling dry, routine procedures day after day. If you're unhappy with your job as it is, you can solve the problem by redefining your role in the organization.

First, look for things that need doing but that aren't being done. Then volunteer to take this work on. For example, let's say you're a technical manager who would rather be doing something else like computer programming. If your department needs to develop engineering software and you're fluent in Java, you could take responsibility for writing the programs. As your department's need for customized technical programs grows, more and more of your time could be devoted to writing the software. By satisfying a need, you've also restructured your job to suit your tastes.

Of course, you can't always write your own job description. Some bosses won't allow it; neither will some corporate structures. If that's the case, more drastic action (such as finding a new job) may be needed to get your career back on track.

7. **Attack problem coworkers head-on.** "All this sounds nice, but not realistic," you complain. "My problem isn't just me; it's the people I work with." Fine. Then you need to assess that source of your job burnout and attack it head-on.

For example, maybe your life is being made miserable by a coworker who simply refuses to cooperate with you. The two of you are supposed to be working on some of the same projects, sharing information and ideas, but your "partner" is a loner who always gives you the cold shoulder whenever you try to get together.

Confrontation is unpleasant, so you could remain silent and try to make the best of it. But you won't be solving the problem; you'll just be running away. You'll only grow more miserable as a bad situation stays bad.

The better tactic is to confront the uncooperative coworker head on. Tell your coworker you have a problem you want to discuss in private. Then, tell him or her your feelings. Explain that you want to do a good job but you can't unless the two of you can find a way to work together productively and without friction. Be direct. Say, "It seems that whenever I approach you, you're not available. Have I done something to make you hesitant to work with me? Is there a way we can get together on this?"

In many cases, the source of our unhappiness at work is another person—a person who is making life difficult for us. By confronting difficult people with the fact that they are being difficult, you force them to admit their poor behavior and take steps to correct it, which makes life easier for everyone.

8. **Change departments.** Sometimes, you can't change the person who is creating a problem for you. Or there may not be another job or task in your department that can provide you with career satisfaction. In that case, changing departments may be the answer.

This is a fairly common occurrence in industry. For example, engineers who would rather deal with people than equations can move into technical sales. A telecommunications specialist who is bored with phones but fascinated by computers might switch to the IT department.

9. **Change employers.** If there's no place in your company where you would be happy, then maybe you should change your employer entirely. The unfortunate fact of professional life is that many places are simply horrible to work; many bosses are despotic tyrants; and many companies are very poorly managed. If you're in one of these situations, the best thing that you can do is to get out as soon as possible. Be sure to keep your job-hunting a secret, and don't quit your present job until you get a new one.

On the other hand, don't rush your resume to the printer at the first sign of trouble. Changing jobs is a major step. Are you sure your problem cannot be solved by less drastic measures, such as a change of assignment, a heart-to-heart talk with the boss, or a week's vacation? Before quitting, try and make things work out. Only when you're convinced that you can't improve your present situation should you put yourself back on the job market.

10. **Change fields.** Changing careers is an effective cure for severe job burnout. If you've had it with what you do for a living, maybe you should do something else.

There are a number of reasons why people hesitate to choose this option. One is the feeling that they studied for a specific career and they'd be wasting their education if they moved into a field for which they were not formally trained. That's faulty reasoning. The real and tragic waste is working at a job that no longer fulfills you.

The second reason for hesitation is financial. People worry that they'll have to take a severe pay cut when they switch fields because they'll be starting at entry level. That's not always the case. True, you may not make as much as you're making now, but you'll probably earn enough to maintain your present lifestyle. If not, perhaps your savings can see you through for the year or two it takes to reach a respectable salary in your new profession.

The third factor that keeps people stuck is that they fear radical change. The change doesn't have to be radical; it can, in fact, be small. For example, a technical writer who is sick and tired of turning out operating manuals doesn't have to join the circus to find happiness. Maybe a different type of writing—say, blogging—will be enough of a change to break the career doldrums.

The decision to change jobs or professions should be made only after a lot of careful thought and soul searching. Change of some kind is definitely called for when you're stuck with a bad case of job burnout. After all, you spend more than a third of your waking hours at your job. Doesn't it make sense to have a job you like?

To avoid job burnout, publisher Dan Poynter recommends taking a week's vacation or getting involved in a totally new activity. Rest and relaxation can help recharge you when you feel burnout coming on. If you have young kids, take a week's vacation with them. If you have a significant other, travel to an exotic, romantic, or exciting place. Or, do a sport or an activity that always interested you but that you never had time for.

The bottom line: If you want to be more efficient and are willing to work at it, you will succeed. If you're not enthusiastic about getting more done and having more time for yourself, you probably won't change the current practices that are keeping you from being fully productive.

Chapter 3

Goal-Setting

The purpose of this book is to help you use your time more efficiently and effectively. Goal-setting can help you accomplish both of those objectives.

When you master the personal productivity and time-management techniques presented in this book, you gain the ability to accomplish more work in less time. When you create a set of specific goals, you ensure that the work improves your career, builds your business, makes you happier in some way, or otherwise achieves your objectives.

The classic study of goal-setting is the one conducted at Harvard between 1979 and 1989. In 1979, a survey of MBA graduates found that only 3 percent had clear, written goals for their future and had made plans to accomplish them. Ten years later, the researchers found that the 3 percent of graduates with written goals were earning on average 10 times as much as the other 97 percent of graduates altogether. This study has been cited countless times as proof that goal setting pays off.

"Living without clear goals is like driving in a thick fog," writes Brian Tracy in *Goals: How to Get Everything You Want Faster Than You Ever Thought Possible.* "No matter how powerful or well engineered your car, you drive slowly, hesitantly, making little progress on even the smoothest road. Deciding upon your goals clears the got immediately and allows you to focus and channel your energies and abilities."

Goals are future-oriented. An excellent way to uncover your goals is to picture what you want your business to look like in a year, five years, 10 years, or even 20 years or longer. Career consultant Valerie Young of *www.changingcourse.com* has her clients write a description of their ideal day; the challenge then becomes accomplishing tasks that move one closer and closer toward living that ideal day every day.

Another advantage of having clearly defined goals is that we tend to move in the direction of those goals once we have them. Without clear goals, we may produce a lot of motion and activity, but it is largely directionless. For example, before completing Valerie's exercise of writing a description of my ideal day, my wife, Amy, and I spent a lot of weekends looking at properties "for fun." With no clear vision of where or how we wanted to live, all we did was look and not buy.

When I wrote my description of my ideal day and read it back, I noticed that it involved me living on the water. Because our children are still in local schools (high school and college), moving to the shore isn't practical for us. The solution: We bought a house on a lake that's only a 45-minute drive from our current home. We also bought a larger four-bedroom instead of a smaller two-bedroom we looked at on the lake, so that, when we are able to move, the house will have plenty of room for us. Once I had the goal, the activity of looking at houses focused and coalesced on buying the property that could allow us to fulfill the dream of living on water, which my wife and I share.

At the time, I was making decent money, but working all the time. I set a goal of having at least $100,000 in net passive income: money coming in independent of my direct labor. A year or so later, I started an Internet marketing business and have since exceeded that goal.

You need not only goals but a plan for their achievement. This plan typically encompasses a series of actions or tasks. Efficient time management is expending effort in the pursuit and achievement of those goals by working on these tasks. Too many of us spend our days handling tasks that, though necessary or pleasing, do not hope us move toward any ultimate goal. Therefore we expend a great deal of time, effort, and energy and do not get the returns we seek.

Let's say achieving one of your goals involves buying a second home now, whether for vacation or as a future residence. You already have a mortgage on your current home. How will you afford mortgage and property tax payments, not to mention repair and upkeep, on two houses? You must have a specific plan in mind. Perhaps rental income from the vacation property will offset or cover the cost of the mortgage. Or maybe you can use an inheritance to buy the second home with cash. Whatever the route you take, you obviously cannot just blindly buy the house with no inkling of how you will afford it.

Again, when you have clear goals and plans for their achievement, you tend to move naturally in those directions. A year or so before we bought the lake house, I did something I had been meaning to do for years and started a second business to generate a spare-time income for us—that Internet business referred to earlier. When we found and bought the lake house, the profits from that second business fully paid the $200,000 down payment and $100,000 in upgrades we made to the house.

A Goal-Setting System

Here is a simple system for setting goals that's especially helpful if you haven't done it before.

There is a lot of talk in the business world today about achieving "work/life balance." The more an employee can balance his or her work and·life, the happier and more productive he or she will be. It is generally agreed by self-help experts that a happy life is balanced in four key areas: health, money, work, and relationships.

Examine that statement and you will see it is true. You can be in peak physical condition and have a great job with a great salary, but, if you have no one to love in your life, you will be lonely and unfulfilled. Likewise, you can have loving relationships, fulfilling work, and ample wealth, but, if you are sick, it dampens your enjoyment of all the other elements. Only when health, money, work, and relationships are in balance can you lead a happy and successful life.

So how do you balance these four elements? Begin by getting four sheets of paper and label them HEALTH, MONEY, WORK, and RELATIONSHIPS.

On each sheet, list as many goals as you can think of. Goals are things you either hope to have or accomplish. These goals must be related to the heading of that sheet of paper. "Find a girlfriend" would go on the RELATIONSHIPS sheet. "Stop smoking" belongs as a goal on the HEALTH sheet. "Get an MBA" could go either on WORK or MONEY. List as many goals, major and minor, as you can think of for each category. Don't stop until you run out of ideas.

Next, put each of the four lists in order of priority, listing the most important goals at the top and the minor ones at the bottom.

Transfer the headings and first three items on each list only to a set of four index cards.

Now you have a dozen of your most important goals, three in each key area of your life, on a set of cards you can carry with you and look at as often as you like.

Here's what a completed set of goal cards might look like:

HEALTH

1. Lose 20 pounds.
2. Be able to run 2 miles.
3. Live to age 90.

MONEY

1. Make $200,000 a year.

2. Live in a million-dollar home.

3. Drive a BMW.

WORK

1. Become a vice president of my firm by age 30.

2. Shorten my commute to a half hour or less.

3. Start my own consulting business.

RELATIONSHIPS

1. Get married.

2. Have two children.

3. Have sex at least once a week.

Between the four index cards, you have a list of a dozen main goals. Why not keep the original sheets with all the goals listed and work toward them all? Because your energy and focus are finite. You simply do not have the time or resources to concentrate on more than two or three key goals in each of the four areas. However, as goals are achieved, you can cross them off and replace them with other goals from your longer list.

Achieving your business goals and making more money may be your priority right now, but you should not exclude the other important areas of health and relationships. Have specific goals for all four areas. When the other areas of your life are all in balance, it makes you happier and more productive at work. Conversely, an individual plagued by personal problems in health and relationships is often unable to work at full capacity and is therefore unproductive.

Goals Should Be Specific

The acronym SMART has long been used to establish criteria for goal setting. SMART stands for specific, measurable, achievable, realistic, and time framed.

Lots of people have vague goals. For instance, "to make a lot of money" is a vague goal. What is a lot of money to you at age 20 may not be at age 30. Also, how do you measure your progress toward that goal? A more specific goal would be "to make $200,000 a year."

The goal must have a metric by which its attainment can be measured. If your goal is to network more actively, by what metric do you measure your success? It could be by the number of networking events you attend per month or the number of new contacts you make as a result of your networking.

Decide in advance what metric you will use to measure your success in attainment of each goal. For happiness, it might be number of vacations you take a year. For some people, it might be the number of times they visit Disney World! Or the number of vacation days or weeks they take per year. Or the number of different countries they visit.

Goals should be achievable and realistic. By achievable, I mean something that is within a person's ability to do. Pole vaulting 60 feet high simply isn't an achievable goal, but pole vaulting 19 feet is for a good athlete.

However, you may not be a good athlete, so although such a goal is achievable, you must ask whether it is realistic. If you are out of shape or confined to a wheelchair, then becoming a pole-vaulting champ is not a realistic goal for you.

You should set a time frame or deadline for every goal. For Amy and me, our goal is to live full-time on the water—at our lake house or elsewhere—within five years. Time frames are important because they give you the impetus to act now instead of later.

The greatest killer of goals is not lack of skill or lack of time but inertia. It is always easier to do nothing than it is to do something. Your goal might be to build your own boat by hand, and your garage has been transformed into a workshop to accommodate the task. When you are tired after a long week of work, though, it may be more tempting to snooze on a hammock in the back yard under your favorite tree than slave away sawing or sanding your boat.

When there is no time frame or deadline, inertia almost always wins, because you can always get to it "later." But a deadline creates a sense of urgency that motivates you to work towards the goal now instead of tomorrow or next week.

Allotting Time for Achievement of Goals

It makes sense that the lion's share of your time be spent in pursuit of your goals. But which ones? Not all goals and the tasks necessary for their achievement are created equal. How do you prioritize?

The Priority Grid ranks tasks according to importance and urgency. The quadrant a task falls into indicates its ability to move you toward your goals.

The Priority Grid

	High	I	II
Urgency			
	Low	III	IV
		Low	High

Importance

In quadrant I are tasks that are highly urgent but not important, at least not in the scheme of things. These are tasks with deadlines that you are expected to complete, such as voting in your town's election or writing an article for your church newsletter. They may be important to others, but they are not important to you. Their completion doesn't bring you the least bit closer to attaining goals of any importance to you. We often jump on these tasks to the exclusion of more important activities. We might be better off questioning whether these tasks really need to be done right away or even at all. Because these tasks are not critical, see whether you can delegate them to others.

In quadrant II are tasks that are highly urgent and highly important. They deserve our time and attention, but do so because they are important toward achieving our goals, with urgency being a secondary factor in time allocation to them. If a task does not contribute to attainment of a goal, perhaps the task belongs in quadrant I instead.

In quadrant III are tasks that are not urgent and not important. Surprisingly, a lot of people spend the majority of their time on these tasks, which include hobbies and socializing. It is precisely because these tasks are trivial and under no deadline pressure that people enjoy doing them. Hobbies are fun and socializing is valuable, but if you dedicate too much time to them, you do so by sacrificing the achievement of some important goals.

In quadrant IV are tasks that are not urgent but highly important. These are the tasks most often ignored by people, precisely because they are not urgent. These are some of the things we must do to achieve our important goals. For example, years ago, to forward my career as a technology writer, I realized it would help me to attain certification in information technology (IT). Staying competitive as a technology writer was an important goal for me, and I believed attaining the certification was an important task in achieving that goal. However, no one was asking or demanding that I do it, so there was little urgency. Yet I signed up for the IT training right away, because procrastination delays the achievement or attainment of the goal you seek.

7 Keys to Achieving Your Goals

Todd Bockman wrote an article at *www.real-estate-online.com* that outlines the seven key steps in achieving a goal.

1. **Desire.** The goal must be something you want to have or accomplish. This yearning must be strong; otherwise, you will not expend the effort necessary to attain it. We *want* lots of things, but we truly *desire* only a limited number of things. You must have a burning desire to achieve the goal, or you likely will not achieve it.

2. **Belief.** You must convince yourself that your goal is both achievable and worth pursuing. Further, you must believe that you are

personally capable of achieving it and that you can learn whatever is necessary to accomplish it. When you look around at others who have attained the goal, you will more than likely find that they are no better or smarter than you are, and your belief that you can do it, too, will solidify. Lack of self-confidence or self-esteem can really get in the way of your pursuit of your goals. The fact is, people who are less talented and not as smart as you have achieved big goals. There's absolutely no reason why you can't, too.

3. **Acquiring the knowledge and information you need to succeed in your accomplishment of the goal.** Thanks to the Internet, it's easier than ever to find the specific information you need to complete various tasks. If you prefer to learn from an expert, read that expert's book, attend one of his speaking engagements, listen to his podcasts, or watch his online video. One of the shortcuts to this step is to find someone who has already accomplished the same goal and model your own actions after him or her.

4. **Getting and taking advantage of the opportunity to take action.** Can you pursue the goal right now? If not, when? What's holding you back? Can you eliminate those barriers? You no doubt can find a lot of excuses as to why now is not the right time or why you can't achieve the goal you desire. Remember the words of Ben Franklin, who said: "People who are good at making excuses are seldom good at anything else."

5. **Having a clear vision of what you want to accomplish.** Pictures can help here. If your goal is to own a new Rolls Royce, clip pictures of the Rolls from the Web and car magazines, and pin them to a board on the wall in front of your desk where you can see them all the time. Bockman notes, "The better you can visualize your goal and its achievement, the better your chances of getting it."

6. **Develop an action plan for the achievement of your goal consisting of daily, weekly, and monthly tasks with deadlines for each.** Use a wall chart or day planner to track the progress of your project.

7. **Committing to the goal's achievement, to persist in the face of adversity and setback.** Here, be guided by the words of Winston Churchill, who said: "Never, never, never give up." Often the closer we get to the achievement of the goal, the longer we have worked and the more discouraged and tired we become.

"Nothing in this world can take the place of persistence," said Calvin Coolidge. "Talent will not; nothing is more common than unsuccessful people with talent. Genius will not; unrewarded genius is almost a proverb. Education will not; the world is full of educated derelicts. Persistence and determination alone are omnipotent. The slogan 'press on' has solved and always will solve the problems of the human race."

CHAPTER 4

SAVE TIME AND MONEY WHEN YOU TRAVEL

This is a collection of tips and ways to save time, money, and headaches when traveling at home and abroad for business or even pleasure (no doubt using the frequency flier miles you collected on company trips). The ideas are based upon the experiences of numerous travelers who have found unique and creative ways to enjoy traveling.

In recent years, airline travel has been severely affected by the combination of the economic crisis and rising oil prices. As a result, airlines are doing everything they can to improve their financial condition and rely on additional fees for checked baggage, preferred seating, and food service.

One foreign airline threatened to charge for the lavatory; they received such a negative reaction that they dropped the idea.

One small U.S. airline, Spirit Airlines, is the not only charging for checked bags but carry-on bags as well. Most airlines don't charge for carry-on bags but do charge for checked baggage with fees that increase, with the number of bags, for both domestic and international flights. Southwest Airlines is one of the few that does not charge for the first two bags but does charge $50 for three or more bags.

Because of the financial strain on the airlines, there has been a significant reduction in the number and frequency of flights to many cities. Thus, the number of seats has declined dramatically, resulting in fewer empty seats on the most popular flights, and even on some flights that were previously uncrowded.

As a result, the best strategy to save time and money on airline travel is to book early—about two to three months before trips for the most popular destinations, particularly at the peak of the season.

If unable to make a reservation several months in advance, try to book domestic flights at least two to three weeks before the travel date. As the departure date approaches, seat prices rise dramatically. If booked less than 14 days in advance, these trips are considered business travel and are priced accordingly.

Saving money on hotel bookings requires a different strategy. If you are attending a conference and wish to stay in the main hotel, book a room as soon as possible. These rooms will fill up early, as they are usually offered at a special discounted price for attendees.

If you are going to a hotel for other than a special conference, you can sometimes find a cheaper room rate as the arrival date approaches. Hotels work hard to avoid empty rooms. If you plan to arrive in a day or so, call the hotel directly, ask for the assistant manager, and see if you can get a room at a lower price or an upgrade, to a suite, at the standard rate. In addition, there are several Internet programs, including *Priceline.com* and *Hotwire.com,* that will bid for a room at a specified price.

Domestic Travel Tips and Tricks

Booking Flights

- Try to make a reservation two months ahead or at least 14 to 21 days in advance.

- Avoid the flights without a weekend in the middle. They are classified as business flights and will cost more. Try to avoid travel dates near and during major holidays, as the best fares are just after the major holidays.

- Avoid the traditional Thanksgiving trip of Wednesday thru Sunday. Instead travel Tuesday to Saturday and save approximately 20 percent on average. Similarly, shop around the Christmas and New Year's holidays for days with lower fares. Flights on Christmas and New Year's day are the cheapest fares of the season.

- Select a seat when you make the reservation or as soon as possible. Airlines may make the exit aisle and bulkhead seating available for a price. Previously, you could obtain these seats at check-in or if you were a high mileage traveler. If you have trouble getting a seat assignment, try the Seat Guru (*www.seatguru.com*).

- Normally, booking a round trip will always be cheaper than two single flights. However, if the airline has special very low-cost single trip fare, it might be cheaper to buy two one-way tickets rather than a round-trip ticket.

- If you discover a lower fare after you have made a reservation, call the airline and explain the situation. Tell them that it is unfair that you could have had a lower fare by waiting. If you are pleasant, they may offer to refund the difference and sometimes will offer a free voucher for a future flight. They rely on the fact that very few people check on fares after reserving a flight.

- In addition to Expedia.com, Obtitz.com, Cheapflights.com, and Travelocity.com, try Kayak.com and SideStep.com, which scour multiple Websites for airline, hotel, and car rental packages and deals.

- Get to the airport early—at least one hour before the flight time or even more, as the security scans can delay the check-in time dramatically. For travel to popular destinations, or during holiday periods, increase the check-in time by another hour.

- Because most airlines are charging for checked baggage, you will save a lot of time by shipping your bag to your final destination ahead of time. It will be at your hotel when you arrive and you will avoid lost baggage, random bag searches, and the checked bag fee.

- You can save time going through the security checkpoint by getting in line with people who appear to be more experienced travelers. However, if you see more than one TSA security person looking at the computer screen, do not get in that line, as they are training the second person, and that will usually really cause a delay.

- Be prepared to remove sharp objects, your shoes, belt, and watch, and anything with a substantial metal content and place them in a bin. Also, remove your laptop from its case and place it in a separate bin. Keep your airport ID (see *www.ifly.com/airport-identification*) and boarding pass available during the security scan. See *www.tsa.gov.*

- Use your business address (or business card) in your luggage tags to avoid revealing your home address and phone number. Tape a card with your name, address, and mobile phone number inside every piece of luggage in case the bag is lost and the outside tag is gone.

- Mark your bags with a ribbon or large bright thread for easy identification, to avoid having someone pick up the wrong bag. Also, remove old airline destination tags, as they're main reason bags get lost.

- Save time on business trips by keeping a packed bag for last-minute trips, fly out of smaller regional airports, book direct flights, select a seat near the front of the aircraft whenever possible, and check in online before going the airport.

- Another time saver is the new Clear Security Pass high-tech card (*flyclear.com*) for frequent travelers at the busiest airports. It requires completion of an online application, an annual payment of $179, and an in-person appointment prior to card activation. The card is back in use after coming out of bankruptcy. It can save you hours of standing in security checkpoint lines.

- If you want to find some airline upgrades, check with CleverDude.com for 10 tips for getting free airline upgrades. Most will be familiar to you, but a few are new and worth checking out.

- Airline lounges offer a more pleasant environment for the frequent traveler and enable you to spend time more productively, or at least in a more relaxed atmosphere. Although the annual membership can cost up to $50, you can buy a day pass for $25 or $50. Delta Airlines will let you use their lounge, for a fee, regardless of the airline you are traveling on. If you are a business traveler, then your frequent flier program will probably offer you free access or membership at a discount.

- A big time-waster for business travelers is the time lost in parking. Whenever possible, sign up for monthly parking passes to avoid the long pay lines. Try to park in the same lot, or at least write down the car location, to avoid a lengthy search when you arrive home.

- If running late for a flight, the fastest way in and out of an airport is to use the parking valet. It's a more expensive service, but can sometimes be the difference between making a flight and missing one.

- Additional travel time-savers include the following: arrange meetings after the peak traffic times (for example, 10:30 a.m. versus 9:00 a.m.), make sure the decision-makers are available (and if not, then schedule another time to travel), and try to combine the trip to meet with another client, interview a job candidate, or meet with a local supplier.

- You can save time and money by using public transportation instead of taxis and tracking the status of your flight on your mobile phone for any last-minute changes. Also, if you need a taxi in an unfamiliar city, use your mobile phone GPS to identify your location and then order the nearest taxi location.

Booking Hotels

- If you plan to use *Hotels.com* for a reservation, make sure to check other sources before you book a room, in order to sample room rates at hotels in the area.

- When planning a last-minute trip and wanting a specific hotel, check with the assistant manager for any special deals and discounts. You may receive a lower rate or an upgrade for the same price.

- If you are a frequent traveler, sign up with the hotel travel reward programs and you will be on your way to a free room and to elite status, and be eligible for upgrades.

- If there is a week or less prior to arrival, try Priceline.com and Hotwire.com to book a room, but be aware that you will not know the hotel or the exact location until you pay. Sometimes, you get a nice surprise with the quality of the hotel.

⊕ Another way to save on hotel rooms is to share a room with two or three people, as long as everyone gets along well. There is little difference in the cost of a hotel room for one person versus two or three people sharing the same room. This usually works well with families.

⊕ Showing up at a very popular area, in season, without a reservation is very risky. Always book these trips well in advance of your visit.

⊕ When booking a room in advance, always ask for a lower rate. There are usually lower rates for AAA (American Automobile Association) members and AARP (American Association of Retired Persons) members. Business travelers, with a business card, can sometimes obtain a lower rate.

⊕ Be sure you know the deadline for canceling a room without a penalty. Some resort locations require 24- or 48-hour notice. Always carry a copy of the booking confirmation, with the reservation number, as proof of the reservation in case the hotel does not have a booking for you.

⊕ Shop around for car rentals, as there are deals at many locations depending on the season and location. Try Travelzoo.com and Carrentals.com, as well as the car rental companies, for any special car rental deals.

Foreign Travel Tips

⊕ Rather than grab the cheapest ticket to Europe, go with the best combination of reliability, economy, and flexibility for your travel needs. Look for tickets as soon as you're ready to firmly commit to flight dates and a destination. If you delay making a reservation, dates sell out and prices generally go up. Special fares are limited to a few seats in order to jump-start departures. It's wise to look for tickets four to six months before you fly. Book your spring and summer travel in the winter months.

⊕ Whether you go online or through a travel agent, plan on spending $700–$1,200 for your round-trip ticket, plus $300–$500 in fuel surcharges, taxes, and other fees.

⊕ Find out when "peak season" begins and ends. At certain crucial times, moving your flight by one day, from a peak date into the next season, could save you hundreds of dollars. Likewise, fares are generally a bit cheaper for travel Tuesday through Thursday rather than on or near the weekends.

⊕ When flying to multiple cities, consider flying "open jaw," which means flying into one city and out of another. In general, the fare is figured simply by taking half of the round-trip fare for each of those ports. It is cheapest when the same airline covers each segment of the round-trip journey.

⊕ Reserve a specific seat for maximum comfort. Most airlines let you choose your seat when you book. To avoid being squeezed in the middle of a row, pick one on the aisle or window, as early as possible. For pointers, see Seat Guru (*www.seatguru.com*).

⊕ Review your ticket carefully when you book it. Double-check your dates, destinations, and the exact spelling of your name. A second look as soon as you get your tickets can give you a chance to fix any mistakes and save you enormous headaches later, particularly if the name on the ticket and passport don't match.

⊕ Check in online before heading to the airport. Most carriers' Websites allow you to check-in and print your boarding pass from home (or from your hotel) 24 hours before departure time. This is a good way to confirm your flight schedule and seat assignment, and it can save you from waiting in check-in lines as long as you are not checking bags.

Booking Foreign Hotels

⊕ In Europe, hotel ratings and prices vary widely. They are not based on room quality but hotel amenities: a new building, classy lobby, 24-hour reception desk, elevator, and high shower-to-room ratio. Budget travelers choose family-run older hotels with hall showers, stairs, and local character.

⊕ Almost anywhere in Europe, you can beat the high cost of hotels by staying in rooms in private homes. You'll pay about $25–$50 a bed at a B&B in Britain (includes breakfast), a casa particulare in Spain, quarto in Portugal, chambre d'hôte in France, soba in Croatia and Slovenia, and Privatzimmer in Germany, Austria, and Switzerland.

- These days, virtually every European hotel and B&B uses the Internet. If they do not have a Website, e-mail the hotel, in simple English, to communicate what you wish for a room. It gives the hotel a quick and easy way to respond, and is free for both parties. If there is no response, the hotel is probably booked.

- When you have been offered a room, that is not a confirmation, and you still must agree to accept the reservation and provide your credit card number as a deposit. If there is no secure Website, you can e-mail your card number or, for a more security, call the hotel or send a fax.

- Request a confirmation with the price quoted. It's smart to carry a printed copy of your confirmation. This will let you keep track of where you're staying and as recourse in the rare situation that the hotel loses your reservation. If you are unsure of your plans, ask about their cancellation policy.

- Small B&Bs, which don't accept credit cards, typically don't require a deposit. However, in places where no-shows are a real problem, some B&B owners request that you mail them a check or wire them money. It is easier, safe, and less expensive to mail a check as a room deposit.

- When checking in, pick up the hotel's business card, as it usually comes with a little map. In many large cities, it is easy to get lost and not be sure of your hotel's exact location. You might even forget the name of the hotel! With the card, you can get a cab and be back to the hotel in minutes.

- In Europe, be aware that "C" can mean "hot." To avoid cold showers, study the particular system, and, before you shiver, ask the receptionist for help.

- While staying in European hotels, leave the key in the door at night so you can get out quickly, if there's an emergency. When you go out for the day, you normally leave your key at the reception desk. Be sure to confirm the closing time, as some hotels lock up at night and expect you to keep the key if you are out late.

Rail Travel Tips

- Rail travel in Europe is quick, comfortable, and relatively safe. Learn to use the 24-hour clock used in European timetables. You can get information on train schedules on the Internet before you leave. The German Railway's Website (*www.bahn.hafas.de/bin/ querey.exe/en*) is the best place to find schedules for trains all over Europe.

- You can pick up free time tables at train stations as you travel. The big, yellow departure schedules are the same all over the world, with four columns that show: destination, type of train, track number, and departure time. Without much effort you can accurately figure it out. If uncertain, confirm your plans with a clerk at the train station information window.

- When deciding on the class of travel, you will meet more local people in second class but find it more comfortable in first class, at a 50-percent-higher fare.

- Make sure you know where to catch your train and where to get off. Many cities have more than one train station.

- Never assume the entire train is going where you are. Each car is labeled separately, because cars are usually added and dropped here and there along the journey. Be sure that the city on your car's nameplate is your destination.

- On an overnight ride, get a couchette—a sleeping berth in a compartment. Make sure to reserve a couchette at least a day in advance with a local travel agency or at the train station.

Mobile Phone Tips

- Mobile phones aren't for everybody. They're often not worth the cost or hassle, if your trip is brief. If you plan to visit several countries in a relatively short period of time, or if you just really want to be on vacation, you can easily get by with phone cards you buy in Europe.

- If you decide to take your phone, make sure it works in Europe before you leave. Some work well; others need some adjustment or may not be compatible with the GSM technology used in Europe.

Money Tips

- It is wise to pay with local cash and not use credit cards. Although credit cards may be accepted in the larger hotels and restaurants, many places offering Europe's best deals—from craft shops to bed and breakfasts—accept only cash.

- When changing cash, avoid exchange bureaus that don't show both the buying and selling rate. If you need cash, you can use ATMs in most cities to obtain the local currency at a reasonable rate, and they're cheaper than using credit cards. Make fewer and larger withdrawals to save money on fees. Many shops will take only cash as payment.

- When you carry cash, wear a money belt and keep it hidden. Take out enough cash for the day, and do not open your money belt except in private.

- Assume beggars are pickpockets. Thieves target Americans because they know we're the ones with the best stuff in our purses and wallets. Be wary of commotions in crowds and fake police officers who ask to see your wallet.

- In any transaction, understand all fees and expenses. Ask to have bills itemized. Do your own arithmetic, and don't let the cashier rush you. Smile and be careful, and you'll save lots of money.

- Make photocopies of important documents you'll be carrying, such as tickets, driver's license, proof of auto insurance, passport, and so forth, as well as a list of toll-free phone numbers for all of your credit cards and bank cards in case they're lost or stolen, or if you need to locate an ATM. Keep a copy with you and give one to a friend or family member.

Chapter 5

The 10% Solution for Increased Personal Efficiency

"We're moving to a culture where everything moves faster, where no one has any time, where we measure out our days not in coffee spoons but in e-mails, beeper buzzes, timed phone calls, children's scheduled play dates, and vacations with cell phones and laptops at hand."
—Esther Dyson, author of *Release 2.0*

Master musicians may have to practice many hours a day, day after day, for a year or more to slightly enhance their skills. In fact, their skill level is so high, they might have to practice this much just to maintain it, let alone improve it. One classical musician commented, "If I don't practice for a day, I know it. If I don't practice for two days, my wife knows it. If I don't practice for three days, the audience knows it."

When it comes to increasing our own personal efficiency, few of us are masters or even close. Therefore, we can achieve significant improvements in our personal productivity—10 to 25 percent or more—without enormous effort. This chapter outlines incremental improvements so you can make tiny "baby steps" that will take little effort, but yield big results.

Feel the Power of 10% More

Stand up. Reach as high as you can. Notice where your hand is? Okay. Now put your hand 6 inches higher.

If you're like most people at my personal productivity seminars, you achieved the increase by standing on your chair or desk. Standing on tiptoes is another favorite method.

The point is simple: The first time we try anything, we usually don't put forth our total effort. So we fall short. To increase your results, then, you can put forth a little more effort than you normally do, just by reminding yourself that's what you need to do to achieve the increased productivity you want.

Let's say you make widgets. You make 50 widgets each hour. Could you do 10 percent more—55 an hour? Probably. Almost certainly. So turn up your motor and do it! You won't need to revolutionize your production methods or gain super-human speed. Just work at it a bit harder.

You'll find it's pretty easy to do 10 percent more of almost anything. Yet this simple effort pays big dividends. In our example, if you work an 8-hour day in your widget shop, a 10-percent improvement will increase yield by 10,000 widgets a year. If your profit is $10 a unit, that's an extra $100,000 in annual profit.

The 10-percent solution can improve your productivity in several different areas. The rest of this chapter will apply the formula to these areas and then offer practical suggestions for implementing the plan.

Increase Efficiency 10%

Do you feel pressured? Do you feel like you don't have enough time even to breathe during the day? "Yes," you may be thinking. But it probably isn't really so. If you don't believe me, try this experiment.

Set up a video camera. Point it at your desk. Turn it on. Tape yourself working. Then watch the tape.

To your amazement, you'll see yourself daydreaming, sitting at your desk staring into space, chatting idly with colleagues, making prolonged personal calls, drinking coffee, fussing with your hair, and doing all sorts of time-wasting, inefficient activities.

While you're caught up in the busyness of the day, you don't mind these things; they're necessary breaks to alleviate stress. On video, they're painful to watch. The tape will clearly show that you can easily cut down on wasted time at least 10 percent without getting stressed.

How can you spend your time more efficiently? An article in *Money Making Opportunities* magazine offers the following tips for increasing the efficiency of your daily routine:

- Create blocks of prime time when you can concentrate on your hardest tasks without interruption. Let everyone around you know that that during these certain hours you are completely unavailable.
- Schedule easy tasks outside of this prime-time block. Writing notes, reading trade journals, filing, and administrative chores can all be done at times when you're not completely focused on a project.
- Keep your prime-time block sacred. If your prime time is 2 p.m. until 4 p.m. don't even think about scheduling a dentist appointment at 3:00. This would break up your block.
- Evaluate the value of each task. Is all this work necessary? Or are you meeting some arbitrary standards that could be bent? You might take a close look at some tasks you thought were necessary and end up eliminating them. Or if someone else thinks these tasks are necessary, let that person do them.

Add 10% More Productive Hours to Your Day

You can't literally cram a 25th hour into a 24-hour day. But you can shift activities and priorities so more time is available for essential tasks.

Many people complain, "There aren't enough hours in the day." When you examine their days carefully, you find that there are more than enough hours to accomplish what they want. The problem is that they're frittering away those hours on nonessential tasks.

The biggest time-waster? TV. No question. A recent Roper poll shows that in the average American household, the TV is on 50 hours a week. Much of that time is spent watching "whatever's on" rather than a specific, interesting program. The proliferation in channel choices has fed this time-waster; couch potatoes can now sit for hours and "channel surf" with their remote control.

If you feel you need the relaxation that "vegging" in front of the TV provides, try the following instead. Sit in your same easy chair. Flip on the stereo or radio to music you like. Let the sound surround you. Have a refreshing beverage and maybe even a snack.

Set in front of you all the materials you want to read but never get to: circulars, direct mail, newspapers, books, consumer magazines, trade journals. Then read them for fun. Have a pen and scissors handy; if an item warrants more careful study or filing at the office, clip it and bring it to work with you the next day. Reserve this time for pleasurable reading only; read only what interests you. Do this, and you will gain relaxation and pleasure similar to what you gain by watching TV without wasting the time.

Gain 10% More Energy

In Chapter 12, I discuss ways to revitalize your mind and body so you have more energy to get your work done.

Before you implement a full program of energy-boosting activities, here are some things you can do to give yourself an incremental lift in energy while you're working:

- Drink cold water, juice, or other fluids throughout the day. Medical experts recommend consuming six to eight glasses of water for a variety of health reasons. Drinking cold liquid also has an immediate, refreshing effect.

- Wash your face. Another revitalizing effect of cold water is its feel on your skin. If you work at home or are lucky enough to have an executive bathroom with a shower, try a mid-day shower. If not, wash your hands and face when you feel yourself tiring. It has a nice wake-up effect.

- Go to bed an hour earlier. Sleep has a restorative effect. If you're just sitting around at night, killing time, consider turning out the lights and going to bed. The extra sleep will pay dividends in increased energy the next morning.

- Eat breakfast—even something small. Personally, I'm not hungry in the morning and the thought of eating breakfast repulses me. On those occasions when I need more energy in the morning, a light snack about an hour after I get into the office helps revitalize me. I can't eat when I get up, but waiting the hour enables me to consume the snack without digestive problems.

- Avoid big meals in the middle of the day. They make you sleepy. "Grazing" is the practice of breaking your food intake into many small increments rather than the traditional two to three big daily meals; some experts think it's healthier. A study in Prague found that people who consumed their daily caloric intake in more than two meals had fewer heart problems. Dr. David Jenkins of the University of Toronto speculates on the Website of the Natural Sciences and Engineering Council of Canada (*www.nserc.ca*) that grazing could mimic the effect that dietary fiber has in helping the body absorb nutrients. In a group of test subjects who consumed their daily caloric intake in 17 small snacks, cholesterol levels dropped substantially.

- Don't drink alcohol during the workday. Alcohol may make you drowsy and impair your mental abilities. At business lunches, order club soda with lemon or iced tea instead of wine or a cocktail.

- Take a multivitamin. Many people are "into" vitamins, minerals, and health foods today, and perhaps you could benefit from such a regimen. Even if you don't have time to investigate nutrition, at least take a multivitamin. That way, your basic minimum daily requirements will be taken care of.

☺ Take a cat-nap. According to *Self* magazine, if your work situation permits it and you feel the need, try a 15- to 20-minute nap when you're really tired. This can be especially effective if you don't get enough sleep at night. Keep the nap brief; longer than 20 minutes or so will leave you groggy for the rest of the day. Don't nap too late in the day; it can make falling asleep at bedtime more difficult (*Self* magazine).

☺ Exercise. Start a moderate exercise program right away: walking, riding a bike, jogging on a treadmill. Exercise for at last a half hour a day at least three days a week.

Get out of Bed 10% Earlier

Don't oversleep. It wastes time and can make you groggy. In addition, if your biorhythm is such that morning is your high-energy period, sleeping late wastes the majority of your most productive time of the day.

How do you know when you are oversleeping? If you wake up naturally—that is, without an alarm clock—and you go back to bed, you're oversleeping. If you use an alarm clock and feel refreshed when you get up, but then fall back into bed because it's warm, dark, and comfy, you're probably oversleeping.

Want a simple, proven way to boost your personal productivity? Get up and go to work an hour earlier every day.

Rather than making you tired, this one-hour early start is an incredible luxury. You can get coffee, check your e-mail, read the paper, catch up on correspondence, or review yesterday's work—in peace and calm—before the office gets frantic.

Waste 10% Less Time

By now you may think I am obsessed with personal productivity. You're right. I particularly hate wasting time. Therefore, I dedicate myself to eliminating time-wasting activities from my life. Do I recommend the same for you? Yes. Time is a limited resource. Once an hour is gone, you can never get it back.

Here is a list of some major time-wasters and how you might eliminate them:

1. **Mowing the lawn.** A high school kid could do this for $10 for you. Why waste the hour or let the summer heat sap your valuable energy?

2. **Raking your leaves.** Same as #1. If you rake because you enjoy being outdoors in autumn, at least wear an iPod and listen to an audio book or seminar.

3. **Shopping.** I rarely go to the mall, preferring instead to sit home and conveniently order products I need from mail-order catalogs and Websites. If you haven't yet tried e-commerce, I recommend it highly.

4. **Gift-giving.** I especially like mail-order shopping during the holiday season. Sitting at my desk with catalogs and Websites at my fingertips, I can get all of my holiday shopping completed in less than an hour. Best of all, once I order, I'm done. The catalog houses and Internet sites gift-wrap my items for me, enclose a card, and deliver them right to each recipient's door. No more midnight runs to the drug store for more ribbons and bows!

5. **Running personal errands.** Running personal errands is a waste of your time. Consider hiring a personal assistant or using one of the many personal services firms that will do this stuff for you. There are people who will do your shopping, prepare your meals, walk your dog, water your plants, and even take your clothes to the dry cleaner for extremely modest fees. Why not try them? Their dollar rate is almost always well below the dollar value of your time. So you gain, not lose.

6. **Cooking.** Shop at today's fantastic value-added supermarkets. You can pick up a wide variety of prepared meals and other value-added foods (for example, cut and washed lettuce, and chicken breasts seasoned and ready for the broiler) that reduce food preparation time virtually to zero.

7. **Housecleaning.** Why every busy businessperson with the income to afford a cleaning service doesn't hire one is beyond me. Housework is pure drudgery and, for most of us, not the best use of our time. Not only does using a professional eliminate this time-waster, but the employees of the cleaning service will go about the task more energetically and enthusiastically than you do—precisely because that's their job!

8. **Making home repairs.** This is another major waste of time. Don't do it unless you enjoy it. You can spend countless hours tracking down problems—a leaky roof, knocking pipe, weak-flushing toilet, odd noise in the attic—that trained professionals can diagnose in minutes. Take advantage of their experience, pay their fee, and save your valuable time for more productive tasks.

9. **Participating in the community.** Only participate in groups—PTO, neighborhood watch, coaching kids' sports teams, church, volunteer fire department—if you believe in their worth and are personally enthusiastic. The more enthusiastic you are, the more you'll put into a group activity—and the more you and the group (or their cause) will gain from your participation. Don't join simply because you feel obligated to do so. Don't go through the motions and sit through the meetings without being a proactive participant—or even a leader—in the group. That only wastes your time—and theirs.

10. **Preparing taxes.** The tax laws are so complex today that it's a mistake not to hire a CPA or other professional to prepare your taxes if you're earning $40,000 a year or more. Yes, some accountants charge a hefty hourly fee. They can do in a day what it would take you a week to accomplish, so even if the hourly rate is equal to or greater than the dollar value of your time, you'll still save. Often, the amount of the refund they calculate for you more than pays the cost of their services.

Think 10% Faster

Thought impulses in the brain are transmitted as electrical signals between neurons. Electricity travels near the speed of light. So thought is nearly instantaneous. Or at least, it should be. Watch people around you. Many are stumped by the simplest questions and can't make even the tiniest decisions.

What's the problem? It isn't that these people are stupid. They just haven't been taught how to think. Thinking, like anything else, is a step-by-step process. It can be taught, learned, practiced, and developed.

The steps of the thinking process are very simple: Identify the problem, assemble all pertinent facts, gather general knowledge, look for combinations, sleep on it, use checklists, get feedback, team up with others, and give new ideas a chance. Once you understand this process, you'll have an easier time making decisions, solving problems, and coming up with good ideas.

Here are the nine steps to better thinking in more detail:

1. **Identify the problem.** The first step in solving a problem is to know what the problem is. Many of us forge ahead without knowing what it is we are trying to accomplish. Moral: Don't apply a solution before you have taken the time to accurately define the problem.

2. **Assemble all pertinent facts.** In crime stories, detectives spend most of their time looking for clues. They cannot solve a case with clever thinking alone; they must have the facts. You, too, must have the facts before you can solve a problem or make an informed decision.

   Professionals in every field know the importance of gathering specific facts. A scientist planning an experiment checks the abstracts to see what similar experiments have been performed. An author writing a book collects everything he or she can on the subject: newspaper clippings, photos, official records, transcripts of interviews, diaries, magazine articles, and so on. A consultant may spend weeks or months digging around a company before coming up with a solution to a major problem.

   Keep an organized file of the background material you collect on a project. Review the file before you begin to formulate your solution. If you are a competent keyboarder, rekey your research notes and materials into your computer. This step increases your familiarity with the background information and can give you a fresh perspective on the problem. Also, when you type notes, you condense a mound of material into a few neat pages that show all the facts at a glance.

3. **Gather general knowledge.** General knowledge has to do with the expertise you've developed in life and business, and includes your storehouse of information concerning life, events, people, science, technology, management, and the world at large.

   In many manufacturing plants, for instance, it is the gray-haired supervisor—the 20-year veteran—to whom the young engineers turn when they have problems. These senior workers are able to solve so many problems so quickly not because they are brighter or better educated than others, but because in their years of company work they have seen those problems—or similar ones before.

You can't match the veteran's experience, but you can accelerate your own education by becoming a student in the many areas that relate to your job. Trade journals are the most valuable source of general business knowledge. Subscribe to the journals that relate to your field. Scan them all, and clip and save articles that contain information that may be useful to you. Organize your clipping files for easy access to articles by subject. You can scan the articles to create a digital library on your hard drive.

Read books in your field and start a reference library. Think back to that 20-year plant supervisor. If he writes a book on how to troubleshoot problems in a chemical plant, and you buy the book, you can learn in a day or so of reading what it took him 20 years to accumulate. Take some night school courses. Attend seminars, conferences, and trade shows. Make friends with people in your field and exchange information, stories, ideas, case histories, and technical tips.

Most of the successful professionals I know are compulsive information-collectors. You should be, too.

4. **Look for combinations.** Someone once complained to me, "There's nothing new in the world. It's all been done before." Maybe. But an idea doesn't have to be something completely new. Many ideas are simply a new combination of existing elements. By looking for combinations—for new relationships between old ideas—you can come up with a fresh approach.

The clock-radio, for example, was invented by someone who combined two existing technologies: the clock and the radio. Niels Bohr combined two separate ideas (Rutherford's model of the atom as a nucleus orbited by electrons and Planck's quantum theory) to create the modern conception of the atom.

Look for synergistic combinations. If you have two devices, and each performs a function you need, can you link them together to create a new invention?

5. **Sleep on it.** Putting the problem aside for a time can help you renew your idea-producing powers just when you think your creative well has run dry.

But don't resort to this method after only five minutes of puzzled thought. First, you have to gather all the information you can. Next, you need to go over the information again and again as you try to come up with that one big idea. Then you'll come to a point where you get bleary-eyed and numb. This is the time to take a break, to put the problem aside, to sleep on it and let your unconscious mind take over. A solution may strike you as you sleep, shower, shave, or walk in the park. Even if the answer doesn't appear, when you return to the problem after a break, you will find you can attack it with renewed vigor and a fresh perspective. I use this technique in my writing: I put aside what I have written and read it fresh the next day. Many times, the things that I thought were fine when I wrote them can be much improved at second glance.

6. **Use checklists.** Checklists can be used to stimulate creative thinking and as a starting point for new ideas. Many manufacturers, consultants, technical magazines, and trade associations publish checklists you can use in your own work. The best checklists are those you create yourself because they are tailored to the problems that come up in your daily routine.

   For example, Jill is a technical salesperson well versed in the technical features of her product, but she has trouble when it comes to closing a sale. She could overcome this weakness by making a checklist of typical customer objections and practicing how to answer them. The list of objections can be culled from sales calls made over the course of several weeks. Possible tactics for over-coming these objections can be garnered from fellow salespeople, from books on selling, and from trial-and-error efforts. Then, when faced with a tough customer, she doesn't have to reinvent the wheel, but will be prepared for all the standard objections because of her familiarity with the checklist.

7. **Get feedback.** Sherlock Holmes was a brilliant detective, but even he needed to bounce ideas off Dr. Watson at times. As a writer, I think I know how to write an engaging piece of copy. But when I show a draft to my wife, she can always spot at least half a dozen ways to make it better.

   Some people prefer to work alone. I'm one of them, and maybe you are, too. If you don't work as part of a team, getting someone else's opinion of your work can help you focus your thinking and produce ideas you hadn't thought of.

Take the feedback for what it's worth. If you feel you are right and the criticisms are off base, ignore them. More often than not, feedback will provide useful information that can help you come up with the best, most profitable ideas. One good guide: If only one reviewer complains about a particular item, you can ignore it. But if all three reviewers make the same comment, they're probably on to something—and you should take a closer look.

Of course, if you ask others to "take a look at this report," you should be willing to do the same for them when they solicit your opinion. You'll find that reviewing the work of others is fun; it's easier to critique someone else's work than to create your own. You'll be gratified by the improvements you think of—things that are obvious to you but would never have occurred to the other person.

8. **Team up with others.** Some people think more creatively when working in groups. How large should the group be? My opinion is that two is the ideal team. Any more and you're in danger of ending up with a committee that spins its wheels and accomplishes nothing. The person you team up with should have skills and thought processes that balance and complement your own. For example, in advertising, copywriters (the word people) team up with art directors (the picture people).

In entrepreneurial firms, the idea person who started the company will often hire a professional manager from one of the Fortune 500 companies as the new venture grows; the entrepreneur knows how to make things happen, but the manager knows how to run a profitable, efficient corporation.

An engineer may invent a better microchip. If she wants to make a fortune selling it, she might team up with someone who has a strong sales and marketing background.

9. **Give new ideas a chance.** Many businesspeople, especially managerial types, develop their critical faculties more finely than their creative faculties. If creative engineers and inventors had listened to these people, we would not have personal computers, cars, airplanes, light bulbs, or electricity.

The creative process works in two stages. The first is the idea-producing stage, when ideas flow freely. The second is the critical or "editing" stage, during which you hold each idea up to the cold light of day and see if it is practical.

Many of us make the mistake of mixing the stages together. During the idea-producing stage, we are too eager to criticize an idea as soon as it is presented. As a result, we shoot down ideas and make snap judgments when we should be encouraging the production of new ideas. Many good ideas are killed this way.

More on How to Get Your Brain to Think 10% Faster

If you still feel slow-minded after deliberately applying these nine steps, you may be losing mental sharpness as a natural result of aging.

The brain is critically dependent upon blood flow and requires one-fourth of all the blood pumped by your heart. As you age, blood flow to the brain can diminish. When that happens, cells begin a breakdown process that eventually leads to their death.

This "brain decay" begins around age 35 and accelerates dramatically when you reach age 50. Your ability to perform daily mental tasks can decline by 30 to 50 percent—and sometimes even more—during your lifespan.

If you're limiting your fat intake, you're even more likely to be short-changing your brain. As you age, your brain actually loses weight—a decline of about 2 percent every decade after about age 40 or 50! To thrive, your brain must be supplied with phospholipids, vital nutrients that are derived from fat. Fat-poor diets can drain the phospholipids supply to dangerously low levels.

To keep your mind nimble, use it often. Do a crossword puzzle. Read a book. Surf the Internet. Go to museums. According to a report in *Science News,* the very act of learning may create a "neural efficiency" in the brain that makes it easier for individuals to think!

You can combat mental fatigue and decline with a physical and mental exercise regimen. Researchers at the University of Pennsylvania Medical Center (*www.med/upenn.edu/news*) believe a lifetime of brain exercise can help stave off Alzheimer's disease, as well as other degenerative brain disorders and a researcher at the Salk Institute of Biological Studies has found evidence in a study of mice that running creates extra brain cells.

Speed Up Your Reading Time 10% or More

As John Naisbitt pointed out in his best-selling book *Mega-trends* (Warner Books), we are in the midst of a transition from an industrial society to an information society. Because of this "information explosion," the amount of reading we must do to keep up in our industry is growing almost daily.

In-baskets and in-boxes across the country are overflowing with journals, reports, papers, memos, faxes, and letters—more material than anyone could possibly hope to digest. Although it's tempting to dump that towering pile of mail into the wastebasket, this is not a practical solution to the challenge of staying informed and competitive in your job. A better idea is to develop a systematic method for dealing with the daily influx of mail.

The following tips can put you in control of information overload, instead of vice versa:

- Be selective in the number of magazines, newsletters, and trade journals you subscribe to or receive. Analyze which give you the best return on your reading time, and cancel those that are borderline, are repetitive, or offer irrelevant information.

- Figure out which sections of each publication are the most useful to you. After reading one or two issues of a journal, you can begin to develop a feel for which columns, sections, and features you should read in careful detail and which ones you should either skim or skip altogether.

- Use the magazine's table of contents to distinguish between useful and extraneous information. If you can't read the articles right away, clip or photocopy items of interest and put them in a folder or in-basket for future reading. This keeps your stack of "must-read material" whittled down to a manageable level.

- Use waiting or travel time to catch up on office reading. Whether you are on the bus or train, in the air, waiting in bank lines, or even on hold on the telephone, these spare moments, normally wasted, can be put to good use by reading.

⊕ Set aside a specific time each day for reading. An hour is usually sufficient. Pick a time when your schedule is relatively quiet and you expect few interruptions. Lunchtime or early morning may be the best period. Keeping distractions to a minimum helps improve concentration.

⊕ If possible, read demanding or crucial material when your energy level is at a high. Some people work best early in the morning, whereas others get more done at night. Figure out when your energy peaks occur during the day, and do your most demanding reading during those times.

⊕ When reading difficult material that requires retention, take notes. Writing down important points aids in comprehension and memorization.

⊕ Take breaks. Studies show that most people can maintain good concentration for about 50 minutes, after which they need a 10-minute break to absorb more information and prepare for further work. Forcing yourself to continue reading when you are mentally tired is ineffective and inefficient, as you tend to reread the same material over and over, and at a slower pace.

⊕ Develop a filing system for saving information on relevant or interesting topics. Five to 10 manila folders will do the trick. For example, if you are an analytical chemist you might have folders labeled "gas chromatographs," "liquid chromatography," "u/v/visible spectrophotometers," and "atomic absorption." This kind of system helps you capture valuable facts and puts them right at your fingertips.

⊕ Set up a system for passing along pertinent articles to others. Give your assistant the names and addresses of friends, co-workers, clients, and colleagues with whom you regularly correspond. When you want to pass along a pertinent clipping, simply tear out the article, attach a note saying, for example, "send to Terry Henderson," and have your assistant do the rest. (If you don't have an assistant, do it yourself!)

⊕ Before you sit down to read for content, make sure you have everything you need. You should have a pen, highlighter, scissors, a note pad or index cards (if you're reading study material), and the complete text of the article.

- When reading trade magazines, tear out the reader service card and keep the card and a pen in front of you as you scan the magazine. By doing so, you can quickly get more information about the products mentioned in an ad or article by circling the appropriate key number on the card.

- Take a speed-reading course or buy a book that teaches you how to read faster. Although most people can benefit from an analysis of their reading habits, this especially applies if you are a slow reader. Do you sub-vocalize (say words to yourself as you read)? Do you read everything at the same speed? Speed-reading can teach you to lose bad habits and develop new, efficient ones through training and practice.

- As a guideline, an efficient reading speed for many types of non-technical materials is between 400 and 800 words per minute. Slower speeds of 150 to 250 words per minute are appropriate for technical material. You may want to improve your speed if you are reading below this level.

Increase efficiency. Make your hours more productive. Gain more energy. Sleep less. Waste less time. Think faster. Read faster. Do these things only 10 percent better and together they'll multiply the improvements in your life many times over.

Chapter 6

Networking Online

Networking has always been a time-consuming task, requiring travel to a networking meeting or event. Now, thanks to LinkedIn, Twitter, Facebook, and other social networking sites, you can now connect with people online in minutes instead of hours, all without leaving your home.

Facebook

What started as a way for classmates to connect, Facebook (*www.facebook.com*) has grown from a social networking site for kids to an on-line venue where adult professionals can connect and do business. With hundreds of millions of users, according to a CNN report, Facebook is

MySpace for business professionals. Users can create personal profile pages as well as pages for their books, create groups, and get the word out about their products and services in increasingly new ways. In this section, we'll take a walk through the site and learn how to use Facebook to promote our businesses.

How to Market Your Business Using Facebook

Copywriter Dina Giolitto writes in a recent article that she started using Facebook about a month ago as of this writing, and it has already resulted in a couple of copywriting projects for her. She shared several tips for using Facebook to promote your business.

Turn Your "Photos" Section Into a Portfolio of Your Creative Work

Most users use the photo section to display their baby photos (guilty) and vacation pictures, but it can also be used by creative professionals as a portfolio of their work.

Use the Status Line as Your "Virtual Sandwich Board"

"Right now, my favorite feature on Facebook is the status line," writes Giolitto. The status line appears just under your profile name as the phrase "What's on your mind?" You can replace it with a sentence or two about what you are doing at that particular moment, à la Twitter. "I've found that a simple line like 'Dina is writing copy for a law firm in California' is a great way to gently remind folks of what I'm all about and how I might be able to help them." You can also use the status line to "share a link, ask a question, express your enthusiasm about something, or share your plans for the weekend." If you're launching a new product or service, or conducting a class or teleseminar, you can share that news as well.

Use Facebook to "E-market" Yourself

There are two ways you can market your services on Facebook. You can use the "invitation" feature to invite your Facebook friends to sign up for teleseminars and other events you are running, and you can create groups that help position you as an expert in your field. "Even if some people on your list never sign up to participate, you're still making it clear what it is that you do and how you can help others," Giolitto writes.

Create Dual Profiles

If your Facebook profile has a mix of personal and professional info, and your friends list is composed of personal and professional acquaintances, be careful what you say and do. Your potential clients probably won't be interested in pictures of you drunk in Panama City, for example. To remedy this, Giolitto suggests creating two separate profiles: one that's personal for your close friends and family, and one that's all business for colleagues and potential clients.

Don't Go "Application Crazy"

When you first create your profile and begin reaching out to friends who use Facebook, you'll receive requests from them to sign up for all sorts of applications, or programs—like widgets—that let you play games like chess or sudoku, answer movie trivia, take quizzes, and give and receive virtual flowers, teddy bears, and other gifts. If you are using Facebook primarily to promote your business, you'll want to keep these things to a minimum. Not only do they clutter up your profile page, but they can confuse visitors, and distort your offerings and possibly even your brand.

Instead, take advantage of the many business applications that Facebook offers. You can find these by clicking on "Applications," and then "Browse More Applications." Useful business applications include one that lets you display client testimonials and one that lets you take a snapshot of your Website to display on your page. There are even apps that will link your Facebook profile with your profiles on other social networking sites, such as Twitter and LinkedIn, as well as your Website or blog. And if you've already signed up for one "What superhero are you?" quiz too many, you can easily delete them from your profile.

Get Personal

Just as with marketing yourself on MySpace, it's okay to get a little personal. Show your human side, talk about the weekend you spent playing with your kids, and share your hobbies and outside interests. "After awhile, you really get weary of being constantly 'pitched to' via email, and Facebook is a welcome relief from that," writes Giolitto. Remember: People buy from those they know, like, and trust. Let your prospects get to know you by showing them the human being behind your product or service.

Twitter: What Is It and How do You Use It?

There is one social networking site that a lot of people are using, even if they don't know exactly why. Twitter (*www.twitter.com*) is a micro-blogging site where users post short, 140 character missives about what they are doing at any given moment. Once you are signed up, you can subscribe to or "follow" another user's Twitter feeds, and they can follow you as well. The site also gives its users the ability to send posts, or "tweets," to the site via their mobile phones.

So what's the big deal with Twitter? Can people actually use it to connect with their target audience and promote themselves?

The answer is yes. In the true spirit of letting customers decide how to use technology, Twitter seems to have been created just so its users can figure out what to do with it. Fortunately they have. Twitter's users post links to their latest blog posts, send messages to each other, and announce seminars, coaching programs, and events.

They also use it post more mundane, often trivial events, such as to announce that they are making dinner or seeing their child's school play, making businesspeople and others wonder, "What's the big deal?" Shouldn't these people stop "playing" and get to work?

In many ways, just as with all social networking sites, they *are* working. Twitter and other social networking sites are what they use to get things done. There's something unique about being able to immediately get in touch with someone right now—a real-time immediacy they can't necessarily do with e-mail or even a phone call. There is even a service called Tweet Later (*www.tweetlater.com*) that allows you to schedule future posts in case you're stuck somewhere and can't get to your computer.

Need another reason to start using Twitter? How about this: Everyone else is.

"Right now I am following Joe Vitale, Seth Godin, and Brian Clark of Copyblogger fame, not to mention other Internet marketers and writers I've met or heard about through other venues," says copywriter James Palmer. "I've only been using Twitter for a few months as of this writing—more to learn what others are using it for than to let the world know that I'm eating a sandwich now—and I've watched people make Twitter a part of their marketing in some intriguing ways. I've used Twitter to track down a couple of interview subjects for another e-book project; copywriter Ben Settle says he uses it to try out headlines. Writers share their latest word counts with each other. Entrepreneurs post links to their latest blog updates or YouTube videos, using tinyurl.com to shorten the URL so their link doesn't go over the 140 character limit. People have used it to spread the latest news, from natural disasters such as earthquakes, to the Amazon.com Website crash a while back. As I typed this paragraph, Twitter was abuzz with the just-released news that Martian soil could grow asparagus."

But is Twitter just another shiny waste of time? Many of those in the know don't think so. Saul Colt, vice president of FreshBooks Marketing, believes Twitter is an easy way to find out what your customers are thinking and doing. "Twitter is here to stay," Colt said in an article in *DM News,* "and in time could be your most valuable marketing tool. There is a good chance your customers are already there and perhaps talking about you, so you might as well get familiar with it ASAP."

Others aren't so quick to tout Twitter as the next big thing in marketing.

Alan Weiss of Contrarian Consulting discussed Twitter and various other social networking platforms in a recent blog post (*www.contrarianconsulting.com/blogs-facebook-twitter-and-chance*), calling Twitter "pretty nonsensical": "Watching someone wash their hair or walk to their car is irrelevant to marketing consulting services. It is idiosyncratic. I think it's fine if people want to do this as a hobby, but for solo practitioners and entrepreneurs, it can drain your life away. It is to marketing what text messaging is to writing a novel."

That may be the case at least some of the time, but many solo entrepreneurs are finding some unique ways of leveraging Twitter for their businesses, even if they need the help of other programs to do so. By using a tool called Summize (*www.summize.com*), for example, you can track what other Twitter users are saying about you, or keep track of what they are doing without becoming one of their followers. Larger businesses that don't want to get involved in Twitter could take advantage of this by tracking references to their company name or latest product, and see what Twitter users say about it, good or bad.

Just like any other social networking Website, you get out of Twitter only what you put into it. So here are a couple of tips that can help you maximize your Twitter experience and keep this site from becoming either a time sink, or something you've started but never used.

Use Twitter to Show People What You're About

I use Twitter to share that I'm working on this e-book or other copywriting project, as well as announce new blog posts. People will probably get bored if you're all business all the time, but new visitors to my profile immediately know what my business is, and many of them decide to follow me on Twitter.

Where Followers Are Concerned, Think Quality Over Quantity

When someone asks to follow you, it is common courtesy to follow them as well, but don't feel you have to follow everyone who follows you. Sometimes they aren't in your target market or are otherwise not a good fit. Sometimes they are only targeting people with similar interests, or are trying to sell their own products and services. You make the call. It's not the end of the world, but if you're using Twitter as part of your marketing strategy, you need to be discriminating about selecting your followers.

When in Doubt, Test

As with all marketing, you should test. Twitter is no different. Are you having doubts about Twitter's validity as a marketing tool? Run a test campaign of Twitter-only offers and see if you get any responses.

Make It Just a Part of Your Marketing Strategy

As with any other social networking site, Twitter works best when it operates in tandem with your other marketing. Use Twitter to announce an event, a new video, and your latest blog posts. Don't close off your traditional marketing channels, either.

Use Other Tools to Help You

Due in part to Twitter's limited abilities, a wide range of software has been developed to help you maximize your Twitter experience. We've already mentioned Tweet Later and Summize, but here are a few more you'll want to take advantage of if you want to start using Twitter with any level of success:

- **Twellow** (*www.twellow.com*). Twellow is a directory of Twitter users, sorted by categories. If you want to find Twitter users in a particular field or industry, Twellow will help you find them quickly and easily.

  For example, I am interested in writing online sales letters for Internet marketers, so I would click on the sub-category "Marketing" under the "Advertising" heading, and look for Internet marketers to follow on Twitter.

  From here, I can search the sub-category "Internet Marketing," and find and follow people as I choose. A few of them will then likely start following me, and can learn more about me and what I'm doing, as well as how I can help them (and I can learn more about what they are offering). Once you're signed up with Twitter, you can add yourself to Twellow's directory by going to this link: *www.twellow.com/user_add.php*.

- **Twitpic** (*www.twitpic.com*). Twitpic allows you to share photos using Twitter. You upload your photos, and the site gives the link a shortened URL à la tinyurl.com and others, for posting in your feed. You can also upload photos from your phone, just like a Twitter post.

- **Twurl** (*www.tweetburner.com*). This site allows you to shorten and track URLs that are posted in Twitter, so you can see how many people are visiting your links. You can even post to Twitter directly from the site. Twurl also keeps track of the top-10 links with the most clicks in the last hour.

  This is perfect for tracking clicks to your videos and blogs and is a must-have if you're going to test Twitter's viability as a marketing tool.

Give Good Content

Remember: People using social media are resistant to any kind of overt advertising. You'll get more subscribers by offering good, information-rich content that helps them solve a problem they're having, than you will by making every post a link to a sales letter for your latest offering. Send your fellow tweeters to helpful videos and articles, and get them into your marketing funnel before trying to sell them something.

Test

As with any other marketing tool, the proof of whether or not it works is in the testing. Run a test campaign of Twitter-only offers to see if a lot of people check out your content, products, or services. Don't discount the other benefits that come from any kind of networking, whether face-to-face or online. You might end up chatting with someone about your hobbies, and that person refers you to someone who needs your services.

Use Twitter to Build Your E-Mail List

When used in tandem with other your other marketing methods, Twitter can be quite powerful, and building your e-mail list is no exception. When someone follows you on Twitter, you'll receive an e-mail message. Visit the person's Twitter page and send him a message thanking him for following you and invite him to sign up for your newsletter. Here's an example: "Thanks for following me on Twitter! Check out my free newsletter at *www.bly.com/reports.*" You can use tinyurl.com or snipurl.com to shorten the link, or use Twurl to track clicks on your link. If your new follower doesn't have his messaging feature on Twitter engaged, visit his Website and e-mail him the old-fashioned way.

As with other social media, you get out of Twitter only what you put into it. I've never heard of anyone getting a client as a direct result of using Twitter, but that doesn't mean it won't happen. Maybe it already has. By being patient, knowing what you want to get out of the experience, and focusing on giving good, useful content and connecting with your fellow Twitter users, I think that ultimately you will find the experience a positive one.

LinkedIn

With an emphasis on business networking, LinkedIn (*www.linkedin. com*) is free to sign up and use, and allows you the options of looking for employment or promoting your business, making it ideal for job-seekers and entrepreneurs alike.

Users can search for people alphabetically or by company, and send them messages. The site also gives users the option of inviting people they already know to join, such as work colleagues and old school buddies.

LinkedIn lets you create a profile that lists your current and past work history, the number of LinkedIn connections you have, your industry, and links to your other online presences, including your Website, blog, podcast, or RSS feeds.

You can also add descriptive tags that, along with the links to your Website or other social networking hub, helps your page rank in the major search engines when people search for your name. I've searched for the names of people and found their LinkedIn profile at the very top of the search results. Sometimes it's the only direct match to the person I was looking for.

LinkedIn also has an "Answers" section, which allows users to ask and answer business-related questions. Sort of an online resume with a few added social networking features, LinkedIn is ideal for professionals and career-oriented people who want to market their services or search for a job online.

There are many special interest groups that have been formed on LinkedIn. An excellent way to gain visibility and make networking connections is through participation in these groups. Here's a time-saving tip: Instead of forming your own group and leading it, join existing groups. Instead of composing original posts on these groups, respond to existing posts. Focus on posts with the most activity, where your comments will be read by more people.

Social Networking in Just 15 Minutes a Day

By far the biggest complain about social networking is that it takes too much time. You have to be careful about becoming a Facebook addict and spending hours online. Here is a plan that can give you the social networking exposure your business and career need in just 15 minutes a day.

1. Set Goals

The first step in launching any social media campaign is to identify your goals. Without a laser-like focus on both the audience you hope to reach and the actions you want them to take, your efforts are doomed.

Fortunately, social networking goals are easy to determine because they are extensions of your broader business goals. All of the things you do in the normal course of work to reach out to customers, prospects, the media, employees, referral sources, and industry peers have social media equivalents. In the physical realm of conferences, networking events, and meetings, you might build relationships in order to capture media attention, drive traffic to your Website, build rapport with clients, or establish credibility with prospects. The online world of LinkedIn, Facebook, and MySpace relationship-building is no different except that you can reach many more people with the click of a button.

Despite the promise of inexpensively connecting with niche audiences, many are hesitant to venture into the unfamiliar, constantly changing landscape of friend requests, tweets, and widgets. Others have leapt in only to see their social media experiments sap time and yield little return on investment. That's why this guide advocates a measured approach: Get more from social media by doing less.

In just 15 minutes a day, you can use social media to follow market trends, build brand recognition, and close sales.

Network to Learn

Many people leap into social networking hoping to profit by driving thousands of online seekers to their Ecommerce sites. That's not a bad idea, but, in the rush to sell, you may miss out on an extraordinary research opportunity. Online social networks, like their offline counterparts, are incredible forums for the exchange of ideas, information, resources, and contacts. By entering a social network with a learner's posture, you're more receptive to the valuable information flowing your way than someone chiefly driven by the desire to sell. Listening to Twitter chatter, observing trends in questions posted on LinkedIn, or following your Facebook news feed can alert you to emergent trends. Then it's up to you to tailor your products and services to meet marketplace demand.

Network to Promote

Online social networks also provide multiple opportunities for you to introduce yourself to niche audiences. In many cases the culture of the network will shun direct sales pitches. You can still profit by increasing brand recognition so that when prospects encounter your business in other settings they are already primed to buy. Answering questions in LinkedIn, distributing links to pertinent industry information via Twitter, or posting commentary on YouTube are all ways to position yourself as an expert and bolster you credibility within an industry. Tactics of this sort also can bring you to the attention of the media. Their coverage, in turn, further establishes your reputation among potential buyers. Remember that it usually takes multiple exposures to your brand before someone buys.

Network to Sell

Once a prospect is familiar with your brand, there's a role for online social networks to play in closing the deal. A well-placed link on your profile page can drive traffic to a sales page on your e-commerce site. A video testimonial from a satisfied customer on YouTube may be just the push a prospect needs to sign up for a service. A recommendation from a colleague on LinkedIn may win a new coaching client. The opportunities are limited by your creativity and focus alone.

2. Choose Your Networks

Just as a billboard isn't the best way to advertise a service for homebound seniors, all social networks won't suit your needs. Savvy Web marketers understand that your time is best spent in the social networks where your key audiences are. A wine distributor might reach out to colleagues via LinkedIn groups like the Wine Business Network or follow wine aficionados via niche social networking sites like corkd.com or vinorati.com. To find the best networks for you:

1. Search massive social networks like Facebook, MySpace, and LinkedIn for groups related to your industry or interests.
2. Check Ning.com, a platform that allows anyone to build a social network to serve any audience, for niche sites.
3. Scroll through Social Media Answer's directory (*socialmediaanswers.com/niche-social-networking-sites/*).
4. Create an online poll asking which social networks your customers belong to and why.
5. Get in the habit of asking your customers, prospects, colleagues, and other professional contacts which networks they use and why.
6. Post a query about social network usage on your blog.
7. Google "best social networking site for [insert your field]."
8. Bookmark and review promising social networks you come across in conversations or via the news.

Once you've identified appropriate networks, you need to spend considerable time getting a feel for each network's culture and capabilities. In some networks you may find it most useful to create a keyword-rich profile so that others searching the site can find you. In other instances, you'll need to reach out to individuals via questions, invitations, and introductions to further your business aims. In still other cases, broadcasting announcements to several contacts simultaneously may be the way to go.

You'll learn what is appropriate only by spending some time in the networks, observing how others interact there, and reading the overviews, FAQs, and other documentation on the sites. To continue with the wine example, let's consider how someone in the wine industry might use LinkedIn, a site with 35 million members in more than 200 countries, and Cork'd, a niche site, differently. The sites' respective features reflect their individual aims and appropriate uses.

	LinkedIn	Cork'd
Create a detailed profile	X	
Invite people to join your network	X	

	LinkedIn	Cork'd
Have a mutual connection introduce you to someone	X	
Send a message to someone you aren't connected with	X	
Request a recommendation	X	
Discuss issues within group	X	
Search, find, and contact group members	X	
Peruse profiles of group members	X	
Catalog, rate, and review wines		X
See which wines others are tasting		X
Track new wines to try		X

Clearly, the two sites offer distinct benefits to users. Their value to you would depend solely upon your objectives. One, both or neither might prove useful in your business now and that status may change over time as the site features and your business evolve. Don't fall prey to random networking. Hold your objectives top of mind and only pursue tactics with a clear tie to your aims.

Also, be sensitive to the way your actions will be perceived by the community. For example, posting great reviews of your own products and bad reviews of a competitor's brand on Cork'd would undermine both your credibility with prospective customers and open you up to widespread backlash. A more appropriate use of this network for a winemaker might simply be to monitor what customers are saying about the brand and learn from it. The depth and nature of your involvement in a social network must vary based on your objectives.

3. Match Network Features to Business Outcomes

After researching various networks, determining which best suit your needs, and observing their cultures, it's time to map out your approach by tying business goals to social networks and specific actions within them. Here's an example:

Goal	Network	Tactics
Position myself as an expert to win speaking engagements and get quoted by the media	LinkedIn	🕐 Include keywords related to my areas of expertise in my public profile. 🕐 Solicit recommendations from people who have benefited from my expertise. 🕐 Answer pertinent questions in LinkedIn Answers. 🕐 Join relevant industry groups. 🕐 Participate in group discussions….
	Facebook	🕐 Post notes on my wall about pertinent topics. 🕐 List upcoming events. 🕐 Optimize profile with keywords….

For each goal, try to identify three to five tactics to employ within each chosen network. This forces you to research each network's features and to think creatively about how they might serve you well.

4. Take Action

As many productivity gurus suggest, what gets scheduled gets done. Create a grid like the one shown here and list all of the tactics that support your goals grouped by social network. Then you can simply set a timer and work your way down the list for 15 minutes a day, or you can create a weekly schedule that reflects the relative importance of different items and the estimated time it takes to complete them.

The following example shows the plan of someone who thinks it is important to update her status bar daily, whereas other items like participating in industry groups or seeking recommendations can be done just once a week.

	Monday	Tuesday	Wednesday	Thursday	Friday
LinkedIn					
Update status bar	X	X	X	X	X
Update profile	X				
Ask colleagues or customers for recommendations		X			
Answer a question in Answers section			X		X
Join industry groups					X
Post content to industry groups pages				X	
Facebook					
Update status bar	X	X	X	X	X
Update profile	X				
Send out friend requests		X			
Join groups					X
Post content to groups pages				X	
Blog					
Post an article or link	X				

5. Monitor Results and Make Adjustments

Spend a couple of months working your plan and monitoring results. In some cases, quantitative measures of success are easily tracked. For example, you can view Web statistics to find out if new site traffic resulted from your LinkedIn profile. Other times hard, fast numbers will prove more elusive.

In either case, rephrasing your campaign goals into questions is the best place to start. To borrow from the prior example, if you set out to position yourself as an expert to win speaking engagements and get quoted in the media, then simply ask yourself: "Have I won any speaking engagements? Have I been quoted in the media?"

This will give you an initial idea of the success of your campaign, but you'll need to take this a step further and get in the habit of asking new customers, media contacts, and other key constituencies how they found you. A radio interview may come as a result of your mom bragging about you in her blog or from your LinkedIn Answers, but you won't know until you ask.

Tweak your plan based on your results and in response to your growing knowledge of social media use among your audience.

6. Automate Updates

Once you've become a pro at reaching your key audiences and yielding desired results, it's time to think about automating some of your outreach. This can compound the success of your initiative by executing more tactics simultaneously, but only if you keep in mind the unique cultures and aims of each network you're a part of and think through your cross-posting strategy carefully. What soars on Twitter may flop on LinkedIn.

The number and variety of online tools that can make your social networking outreach more comprehensive and efficient are increasing all the time. Here are a few automation options to get you started:

- **Ping.fm:** This site allows users to send text and images from mobile phones, e-mail, instant-messaging services, and more to be posted on more than 30 different social networking sites. You simply create a user name and password; add the social networks you are a part of; type messages, or upload photos; and select the networks you want them posted to.

- **FriendFeed.com:** This site can streamline your social network reading by bringing all of the Web page, photo, video, and music updates of your friends and family across social networks together in one interface.

- **Scoutle.com:** This site automates the process of finding and connecting with bloggers who write on similar topics. It allows users to create personal Web crawlers, called "scouts," that search the Internet to find other "scouts" that share its subject area, language, geography, or other factors. From there, it compiles lists of suggested interesting blogs, which you can then recommend, join, or create networks with.

Chapter 7

Using Technology to Save Time

Let's face it. You don't want to start your business and realize you have a computer so outdated that you spend more time trying to fix it than actually doing business with it! Time lost to fixing your computer means dollars lost that could have been in your wallet a whole lot faster!

When you get ready to roll with your business then you want to be sure you have the best technology you can manage to buy already set up in your home office. You might question which way is the best to go for a computer first: desktop or laptop. Ask yourself how mobile you are on a daily basis, and consider whether having a portable laptop would be the best arrangement to begin with. Laptops are always useful, even to just sit on your lap while watching television and you can still surf the Internet, looking for information—even that which you see on the television and want to know more about.

For instance, if you are moving around all day long, you can stuff your laptop into a shoulder bag along with your mouse, headphones, and electrical hookup. Don't have Internet access yet? Go to any Borders or Barnes and Noble bookstore and see if they have a coffee shop where you can sit and use their free Internet service. Many other locations, including Starbucks, hotels, and even McDonald's, offer free wireless access these days. You will, however, need to make sure you have wireless access built into your laptop. All new laptop models now have wireless installed, including those manufactured up to about three years ago. Before that, laptops needed to have a wireless modem plugged in for surfing the Net.

With wireless installed in your computer, you can just turn on your laptop, click on your Internet access link, and the open (unsecured) Internet service available for your area will open up and ask you to agree to service use terms, which you will then accept. From that point onward, you can surf to your heart's content. Be advised, however, that these types of open Internet access services are *not* secure so you may not want to exchange sensitive personal information online (for example, credit card numbers, social security numbers, computer pass codes, and so on), such as when paying bills. You will also be prevented from accessing certain sites like pornography or e-mail sent through Outlook Express. Yahoo and Google mail accounts, however, are just fine to use.

The big bonus in working at your local bookstore is that, if you need to search for detailed information, then there you are, at your very own library, with thousands of books right at hand for you to pick up and take to your coffee table. You don't have to purchase those books, although if you spill coffee on one, I suggest buying it as a courtesy. You messed it up, so you should buy it.

Another good point about your "traveling" office is that you can also scan information bits into your computer while at the bookstore, as long as you use a small but efficient scanner that fits in that same carry bag. Be aware that scanning small chunks of information is fine, but if you think you need a lot of information from that book, then you should just buy it. Or purchase an online version of the book, which you can download right to your computer. Time saved. Or just go to the library and see if you can check it out there if you don't want to spend the money.

Equipping Your Home Office

If you plan to be sitting in your home office on a daily basis and maybe don't have the need for a mobile laptop, get yourself a desktop or tower computer, which you can set under your desk, with the viewing monitor on top of the desk at about eye level. Install a keyboard drawer that slides out from underneath and allows your hands to rest in just the right place to type for any length of time without straining your wrists and hands.

Buy yourself a very comfortable, padded swivel chair that has options to raise or lower itself according to the right height you need for your hands to type comfortably on the keyboard. Your feet should both rest comfortably on the floor, and you should hold your back straight up to do any typing. You might have to experiment to find just the right seating position for your body that will allow you to comfortably type for extended periods of time.

You also want to have your monitor about eye level or slightly above, looking straight forward, so as not to get neck and shoulder strain when sitting for a long time. Avoid looking down, which, over time, will strain your neck and upper shoulders. This is part of "ergonomics," which is the proven concept of using your equipment in a manner that avoids physical strains and other discomforts that occur when sitting for a length of time in one position.

How do you find the right computers and additional gadgets? Start by studying the Sunday paper for insert ads from Best Buy and any other stores that offer electronics on sale. Fry's is also a great one where you can get new computers, printers, fax machines, mouse and keyboards for cheap, *and* buy parts for your computer if you are talented enough to be able to manually upgrade your current one on your own. Once you've studied what computers on the market have installed today and for what range of prices, then you can compare between sellers where you can get the best bargain.

You can also take a little risk by going down to your local pawn shops and checking out what they have on sale. Oddly enough, I got my last laptop from a pawn shop and got a great deal on it! It happens. I know it was new because when I first tested it, I had to set up everything in the computer in order to get it running, and it had all the warehouse wrappings still on. I then put it on layaway for two weeks and then went back and got it out. (No, it was not a theft item because the police will always check these things out. It's part of the pawn shops' arrangement with the police. Pawn shops really try to avoid taking in stolen items, and are required to wait 21 days before the items can be pulled out of the vault and sold.) I imagine that someone had a surplus stock from a wholesale arrangement and brought them in to the pawn shop to just get rid of the stock. It pays to know people in all the right places who can tell you where there's a bargain deal! Keep your ears open.

What about printers, fax machines, and telephones for your office? For a printer, you need to buy one that prints what you need on a regular basis. If you are sending out business letters through snail mail (regular postal), then you might need something very professional that looks good and gets your reader's attention. Check at your local stores to see these printers, especially if they can be shown in action.

Be aware of your printer cartridge set-up. Some printers have all the inks in one big container and when one runs out, you've got to change the whole thing! Very expensive! Go with a printer that allows you to change one cartridge color at a time as it runs out but still prints well. Also check how fast a page is printed. You don't want to be sitting for 30 minutes, waiting for a 20-page document to print out, especially if you are trying to get to an appointment. This is especially true for larger, better-quality thermal printers, usually found in company offices. Though expensive, this type of printer may give you a return in investment (ROI) over a period of time just in cartridge use and speed of printing. It will also break down very rarely.

If you think you need a fax machine and a scanner, then you might want to consider getting an all-in-one machine that prints, scans, and faxes. It depends what you need in terms of documents that must look a certain way and will be distributed manually in a professional environment. Or you might just need a printer and can use a software program to do all the faxing for you. That is probably the easiest way to go, but, again, it depends on your needs.

Designing Your Office

What should really be decided before even setting up your equipment is how everything will be placed in your office so that what you need is easily accessible from your seated area. Designing your office layout first is crucial when you consider where you want to sit in the room; where natural lighting, if any, affects your working area; and what type of electrical outlets are available to handle all your equipment safely and efficiently. Investing in electrical cords with five to six plugs, ones that are shock-proof with reset buttons, will be a big help in consolidating your equipment closer to your sitting area. You can also check out the latest in electrical safety equipment that allows you to plug almost everything into one apparatus and protects against electrical surges. Still, spreading out the electrical loads and hookups is a much safer way of protecting your equipment, if you can do it that way without tripping over wires.

Adding more light over your seated work area is very important so you avoid eye strain from constantly looking at the monitor screen. Additional defusing overhead lighting arrangements safeguard against screen glare, which is more concentrated and tiring for your eyes after a while. Take breaks often so your eyes stay relaxed.

Next, you want to decide where the desk, lamps, computer(s) (laptop and/or desktop) will sit, where monitors are placed so there is no glare from available lighting, and where a printer/scanner/copier can be located without taking up too much space. If you do a lot of scanning, you can create a three- or four-shelf arrangement that allows you to set a scanner, fax machine and a printer, all in one consolidated containment area by your desk. Each item sits in its own cubicle but with plenty of overhead space for each to lift the lid, load paper, change printer cartridges, all without going through some rigorous song and dance routine to get the job done. Make your office, and access to all you need, as easy as possible so it is enjoyable to work in your area. When you are comfortable, you will get more done. That means more money coming in faster, too.

Then decide if you need filing cabinets and determine where they will go in the room. If you don't need to access them often, then put them farther away from you in the room or even in your garage, particularly if you are just storing your materials after a completed project. Put your primary bookshelves closer to your computer station so that you can easily access any reference books and materials you need to grab at a moment's notice when you are seated at your workspace.

Once you know where everything is going in your new office, then you can really plan what you need to have in the office in terms of an office computer: gigabyte (GB) memory, processor chip, graphics card, and random access memory (RAM). If you are a desktop designer and use heavy graphic programs such as Adobe Photoshop, Microsoft Office with extended components such as Access, Publisher, and any other memory-consuming application, then you'll need to find a desktop with a heavy-duty graphics card, or have one installed after purchase. You will also need the latest in processor speed and plenty of hard drive memory (222 GB, for example).

Your monitor, usually purchased separately, must also be able to handle high output graphics, too, so ask questions of your salesperson while you're out shopping around. Additionally, 3 GB of RAM is pretty standard now in most computers, including laptops. Don't get anything less than that for your starter computer. Some laptops currently come with 8 GB of RAM at this writing.

Specifications and design are changing almost monthly in the computer business, but there are ways to also upgrade your equipment as time goes on. Adding more RAM will add speed processing to your computer. If the computer you have now is five years or older, you can also call a computer technician or someone from the Geek Squad who can talk to you about what you have and how much it would be to upgrade it. You might decide to just make it a second computer for lightweight applications like text documents, and then splurge on a new generation desktop computer.

With regard to hard drives, the one installed in your computer should be more than 222 GB in a laptop and even higher in a desktop tower. Note: If you decide to purchase a Netbook, which is smaller than a laptop, then 160 GB for the hard drive and 1 GB of memory is fine for starting out.

Using Netbooks

The Netbook is mainly a communication device, rather like the Droid phone but without the steroids, and yes, you can work on files. The problem is the keyboard, which is on the small side—somewhere between 7 and 10 inches wide—so there is a large room for typing error, particularly if you have large hands and fingers. You might be fixing many typing mistakes rather than spending time doing the work you need to get done!

Most screens on Netbooks now have respectable resolutions of 1024 x 600, like regular laptops, but the problem is in sizing the page to fit onto the Netbook screen when the resolution is less than that. In a number of situations, you will need to scroll from side to side in order to see a whole sentence, and that can be quite annoying when reading a large article or downloaded book.

One other note about the Netbook is that it does not come with a DVD-CD player. You would need to purchase that separately as an external player and connect through a USB port. Most Netbooks have one or two USB ports. You can add on an external hard drive as well to store most of your information and to transfer it to other computers.

The main attraction of the Netbook is that it is more like an extension of your home computer communication systems, able to perform quick, easy functions but not intended as a heavy-duty performer on graphic programs. If you mainly use a computer to access friends on Twitter, Facebook, MySpace, and other social media sites, then this is a great tool for you! Also a great-to-have feature is Skype, a "Voice over Internet Protocol" (VoIP) program that allows you to make free calls to another person with the Skype software installed. If you are making calls from Skype to cell phones or land line phones, then it will cost you a little bit of money. (Go to *www.skype.com* to find out more about using this program.)

Picking Peripherals

If you have now decided on what kind of computer you want to use, then it's time to decide on a mouse and keyboard. Most desktops will come with their own keyboard and a mouse, both of which are fairly standard and just fine for most applications. You can replace both with wireless keyboards and a wireless mouse, which are great to use and usually have additional features and benefits the standard ones don't offer.

If you do that, then also purchase one AA/AAA battery charger for around $30 and maybe eight to 10 rechargeable batteries. Wireless devices use batteries, and you will find it expensive if you are just using the basic high-level AAA batteries, which will go out after two weeks of daily usage. If you have the rechargeable kind, then you can keep your batteries rotated. When two have been used up, take them out, put them in the charger, and pull two others out from storage. Replace them in the mouse and you're ready to go again in just minutes!

It's worth the expense to have a battery charger with spare batteries. Energizer® sells a great AA/AAA charger, and you can purchase eight-count packs of rechargeable batteries in the same line. Always stay with the highest grade of rechargeable batteries you can get. (As an aside, if you are a photographer using a digital camera, these batteries work great in them. Regular batteries usually run out very quickly, so either use the rechargeable ones or invest in Energizer Advanced or Ultimate Lithium batteries, which give you the highest performance with your digital camera. They are not rechargeable, though.)

Last, but not least, invest in a sound system for your computer. Usually there is the basic speaker arrangement installed on a laptop. Some desktop towers can use a monitor with speakers already attached but it is usually best to just find a good speaker set-up that you can plug into the tower and have stereo surround sound. It is great to be able to listen to your favorite music pieces while working on one of your projects—as long as it is not interfering with your concentration.

Also, listening to conference calls and webinars from your computer is great! You can attend a meeting online, listening to what is being said, while you continue to do things around your office. If you need privacy, invest in a good set of headphones so you are cut off from outside noises and distractions. You can find what works best for you: a little background noise or absolute silence in order to complete your work. Additionally, you might want to invest in a headset with a microphone added, which allows you to call over the Internet and be heard very well.

Backing Up Your Hard Drive

One of the most important parts of setting up any of your computers and filing systems is having a good system of backup. There are several ways to do this. One is to back up your computer to an online service where you can access it anywhere in the world that you can get on the Internet. There are several online companies that provide this service for a fee. Check over each one of them to see what services they offer, and make comparisons according to what your needs will be. (One is *www.mozby.com.*)

Another way to do backups is to do one full backup of your whole system online or onto a large portable, external hard drive that simply plugs into a USB port located on your computer. Then back up project files that change on a daily basis to be sure you never lose your clients' work. There are many smaller backup drive plugs about the size of a lighter that range from 2 GB and up which you can plug into your laptop. They can be easily carried in your pocket or in a small container in your computer bag. Invest in several of these so that you can always back up files on the go.

You can also simply burn backup rewriteable CDs on your CD-DVD drive and just use them over and over again until you are ready to archive everything onto a permanent non-rewriteable CD. Believe me: You do not want to ever have a problem with your computer where all the data disappears, no recovery system was ever set up, and you don't have a second copy of the client's project. It could mean hours of work down the drain and dollars lost to you as you try desperately to re-create everything from memory. It takes only one time to learn this lesson, and you will never forget it!

Organizing Your PC Files

You have made all your purchases, hooked everything up, and are now ready to work. There is one feature of using a computer that we have not discussed yet: how to set up your file folders on your computer so you know where everything is.

When you turn on your computer for the first time, note that there are folders already set up such as "My Documents," "My Pictures," "My Videos," and "Library." You can go to "My Documents" and start setting up your own office files. For example, you can create a series of new folders for parts of your business. Here is a sample of what you can create.

Home Office (main folder)

Subfolders: (You create all these folders inside the "Home Office" folder.)

- ❏ My Financial
  - ■ Bank #1 (created folder inside "My Financial")
    - ○ Checking (created folder inside "Bank #1")
    - ○ Savings (created folder inside "Bank #1")
  - ■ Bank #2 (created folder inside "My Financial")
    - ○ Checking (created folder inside "Bank #2")
    - ○ Savings (created folder inside "Bank #2")
- ❏ My Marketing
  - ■ Brochures
  - ■ White Papers
  - ■ Client Letters
- ❏ Copywriting Projects
  - ■ Client #1
    - ○ Barnes & Noble Promotion
      - ● Diversity Book
  - ■ Client #2
    - ○ Beach Party Ad
      - ● Night at the Ritz Event
- ❏ Picture Projects
  - ■ A Day at the Zoo
  - ■ Riot on Main Street
- ❏ My Personal
  - ■ Love letters from my hubby

- ■ Mom's e-mails from Europe 2008
- ❏ My Jewelry Store
  - ■ The Wedding Line
  - ■ Biker Jewelry Line
  - ■ Plain & Simple Line
- ❏ My Webs

Organizing all of your files as you build them will be extremely important. If you have a system set up like the example here, then you will know where to put everything as it is created. Keep loose files off your desktop, as it is distracting to look at all those little folders after two weeks of saving them. Now you don't even remember what most of them contain! That means you've got to spend time opening each one up so you can figure out what folder to put it in, or if you have to make a new directory folder for it. What you can do, however, is create a desktop folder and put shortcuts to all your files in that folder. As you work during the day, you can have that folder minimized, then opened to slide a finished document onto the shortcut for the filing department where you want it to be stored.

If you are new at doing downloads of materials to your computer, in most cases it will automatically save to "Downloads" in your directory. You can always create the same kind of filing system in "Downloads," but you will need to actually select the sub-folder your download should be saved in.

Choosing an Internet Provider

Everything is set up at home in your office. Now you need one last piece of the picture put into place: your Internet connection. Here's where you really need to do some research to determine what you need. If you or the whole family like to watch television, then maybe a package deal like AT&T's Uverse system will work just perfectly. You have all your regular channels and, depending on what level of access you want, you can get tons of channels devoted to movies, sci-fi, history (my favorite!), science—almost anything you want. You can also limit access to the children through parental control systems and make sure they are not ordering pay-per-view movies right and left while you're not looking.

Part of the Uverse package also includes Internet, access which you can get at different levels of speed. I would recommend getting a high level of it, especially if you are on the Internet often doing research and need to access sites quickly and efficiently. By the way, make use of the "Bookmarks" tag on your Yahoo or Google toolbar at the top of your Internet program, usually found on Microsoft's Internet Explorer. You can also download the toolbars and add on components to help you work faster at getting from place to place on the Internet. Don't you just love technology?!

The last part of your Uverse package may include a home phone that you can use for your phone calls. There are several different arrangements for that, and you need to decide if you need it, or, if you do, whether you need unlimited local calls only or a full service for an additional monthly fee.

There are a number of different companies offering the same kinds of deals but in different arrangements so you would need to decide if you want satellite, cable, or any other arrangement that might be cheaper, provide only Internet, or have other neat amenities that Uverse might not offer.

Another aspect to consider with Internet and television access is where you live. Though most cities now have access to everything, some people who live in the countryside—or even some suburbs—can only get certain types of services due to the companies' coverage there. If you have a laptop handy, you can go into the city, sit at a bookstore, and access their Internet. Then pull up a list of services by doing a Google search on "Internet Access."

A list of companies comes up, and you can check each one on their site by plugging in your zip code to see if they offer access in your area. If not, then move on to the next company. When you hit a company that does offer in your area, study their packages first to have a good idea of what's involved before calling them. One thing: Don't let them sell you too many services right off the bat. Start simply but efficiently, and then move up to a higher package if you really like the service. Make sure you can move up too before agreeing to any contracts or arrangements. I also recommend getting a package that you just pay for on a monthly basis, with no contracts. That way you are not signing away your life—or your credit—if something goes wrong!

With this information, you can get your office started, organized, and up and running within a very short time. The quicker you have everything planned out, set up, and ready to go, the faster you will bring in the money you need to build a strong business! Have fun! Check the following links for more information so you can make better choices.

Useful Links

Information on Computers, Laptops, Printers, and Peripherals

www.CompUSA.com

www.frys.com

www.bestbuy.com

www.pcmag.com (Reviews and notifications on the latest and greatest on the market.)

www.computerworld.com (More technical information.)

Online Backup Services

www.barracudanetworks.com (Online backup services.)

www.ibackup.com (Online backup services.)

www.IronMountain.com (Online backup services.)

www.dontloseyourdata.com (Reviews on online service companies.)

www.consumersearch.com/online-backup-services (More reviews.)

Upgrades and Repair

www.bixnet.com/laptopupgrade.htm (Need to upgrade your laptop? Go here to find out more information about your laptop and what options are available for upgrading. This site covers processors, hard drives, and other components.)

www.daileyint.com/hmdpc/upgrade.htm (Look here for information in upgrading laptops—what you can do and what you can't. Laptops, in general, are much harder to upgrade than desktop towers.)

www.geeksquad.com (This group can help you if you're having problems with your computer. Find out here what services they offer. You can also visit a local Best Buy electronics store to find out more information. Geek Squad is Best Buy's choice for repair services and will make home visits when needed.)

www.pcworld.about.com/od/computers/5-Easy-Hacks-for-Your-PC-and-W.htm ("5 Easy Hacks You Can Do on Your Computer to Upgrade It Without Spending a Dime"—great article for computer literates who want to do the upgrades themselves)

Netbook Information Links

www.gottabemobile.com (Covers Netbooks, laptops, tablet PCs, and has great information for the newbie.)

www.blog.laptopmag.com (*LAPTOP Magazine*'s blog area where you can learn the latest and greatest news about Netbooks, laptops, etc.)

www.liliputing.com (Liliputing [for the smaller laptop] has the latest in Netbook information and news releases.)

www.trustedreviews.com (Provides very direct, no-frills reviews on laptops and other electronics.)

Miscellaneous

www.magicjack.com (Learn how you can make phone calls from your computer for very cheap! Great product, but not great customer service.)

Chapter 8

Going Mobile

Not too many years ago, the fixed landline telephone was considered the most modern communication device available and used by most people and business. After 10 years of hearings, the FCC finally approved modern cell phone technology in 1982.

With the evolution of the cell phone, satellite phones were subsequently developed for use where cell phone towers were unavailable and landline systems were too expensive to install, particularly in smaller, less-developed countries.

Since then, mobile communications technology has exploded dramatically in ways that were not anticipated a few years ago. The technology includes both the Internet and mobile communication usage and devices.

Not too long ago, Internet communication involved video and voice communication, e-mail, instant messaging, and Skype communication. Now there are Twitter, Facebook, LinkedIn, and others coming soon.

Today, mobile communication devices include both the numerous Internet communication software offerings closely followed by the evolution of the cell phone into the smartphone.

Expanding Technology

As a result of increased usage and demand, the technology continued to evolve with the development of 3G networks that are now considered as the standard. Recently, a 4G network has become available, offered by a few telecommunication companies to accommodate the increased usage of data communication.

In the early years, cell phone usage was somewhat limited to relatively few users. The phones were expensive, fairly large, and referred to as "bricks" because of their size. In the 1990s, when 2G networks were developed, the second-generation cell phone came into wider usage as the cell phones became smaller, more compact, and handheld devices, and the network bandwidth expanded to permit a greater number of users.

Today, cell phones have become so common that children believe they have been deprived if they don't have one. When children are given their own cell phone, parents have better and timelier communication with their children. But at a price! Parents soon discover that, unless they have purchased a cell phone contract with unlimited usage, the text message charges can really mushroom. It is not unusual for a teenager to bill hundreds of hours worth in text message charges in a few weeks.

Mobile phones have revolutionized modern communication and have empowered consumers and business users alike. The advent, acceptance, and proliferation of mobile phones have expanded the opportunities and possibilities for millions of people. Rural, hinterland, and underserved areas are now interconnected to urban areas due to cellular communication technologies.

Mobile Phone Usage

Mobile phones can be used to give alerts or early-warning alarms for a wide variety of emergencies such as a medical crisis, weather-related disasters, accidents, and crimes.

As the global usage of the Internet expanded in recent years, so has the use of cell phones and smartphones. Today it is not unusual to see someone walking along and, apparently alone, talking out loud when in fact they are connected to a cell phone via a Bluetooth earpiece.

Mobile communications have grown rapidly throughout the world as an important part of the expansion in global business. This is because the use of mobile communications increases business productivity with simplicity, efficiency, and transparency as the primary objectives.

Historians of telecommunication technology will probably refer to the years between 1997 and 2007 as the decade when companies began to integrate their telephone and data systems as a method of reducing cost and increasing efficiency.

Evolution of the Smartphone

If you haven't heard of smartphones, you are one of the few. In recent years, we have experienced a rapid evolution of smartphones in the global cell phone market. As the name suggests, smartphones are meant to be smart. What exactly is a smartphone, and how smart can it be?

Essentially, smartphones are cell phones plus a variety of additional functions. These functions expand the ability of traditional cell phones to perform far more useful tasks than to make and receive phone calls and messages. Enhanced with the advanced Internet-based technology, a smartphone works as a portable digital device or a mini computer that you can carry anywhere.

With a smartphone, in addition to the original purpose of making phone calls and sending messages, you can experience e-mail capacities, manage your personal and office documents, visit Websites for up-to-the-minute financial information, search for information, play online games, read news, and so forth. In addition, smartphones can be synched to your PCs or laptops, able to share and load documents or applications with each device.

It is widely recognized that smartphones have increased people's ability to acquire information faster and made life easier, which explains why so many people are willing to spend big money for such a small device.

In the chronology of mobile phones, smartphones are a combination of cell phones and personal digital assistants (PDAs). Originally, cell phones were only used to make phone calls, just like landlines. The biggest difference is that a cell phone is wireless and completely portable, whereas a landline phone is hardwired and restricted to its primary location.

Eventually, mobile phones were expanded to include messaging function. At the time, handheld personal digital assistants, such as palmtop computers, were limited to be use for computer technology-related functions including the management of files, contact information, agendas, taking important notes, and so on. In addition, a typical PDA had Internet access with Bluetooth and Wi-Fi capability, including access to e-mails.

Smartphone Features

The principal features of today's smartphones include an operating system, a touch screen, a number of software applications, Internet access, e-mail messaging, and the ability to synch with computers.

Every smartphone is designed with an operating system (OS) that enables the use of software applications designed for specific smartphones. For example, iPhone from Apple runs on the iPhone OS, and BlackBerry on the BlackBerry OS. In addition to the basic software applications of most ordinary cell phones, including an address book, contacts organizer, and a calendar, the smartphone includes substantially more sophisticated software applications.

Many popular software applications have been incorporated in the majority of smartphones, including document and photo viewing as well as editing capacities, a GPS mapping device, and application download capacities. The most useful feature is the ability of most smartphones to connect to the Internet, as a result of the development of 3G technology and Wi-Fi networks.

Although some smartphones cannot provide fast access to the Internet, they all provide some sort of Web access. In addition, their computer synchronization ability makes smartphones very useful in that they can share many documents or software applications with any computer.

With synchronization, you can use a computer to manage some of your smartphone tasks, such as organizing your smartphone contact information on your computer, which is easier to use. As the technology of smartphones develops constantly, we will see the emergence of more and more smart features that will make them even more useful.

What's Driving Smartphone Growth?

Demand for smartphones continues to increase. Innovative smartphone designs with more user-intuitive features, such as touchscreens, as well as widespread rollouts of 3G networks have increased speeds dramatically, improving the experience of using mobile browsers and applications.

In the corporate environment, smartphones have been must-haves for years, streamlining business processes with instant access to valuable information. With increased speeds and functionality, smartphones have become so integral to competitiveness, by boosting productivity and increasing efficiencies, they are considered an essential tool for every salesperson, manager, and executive, even during these budget-slimming times.

Wi-Fi Capability

Some models of BlackBerry and iPhone, as well as other smartphones, are Wi-Fi capable and allow you to access the Internet when you are in the range of a Wi-Fi network.

Over the past five years, mobile computer users have benefitted and, to a significant degree, have relied on wireless high-speed connectivity in the home, office, and various "hotspots" around the globe, whether their local coffee house or an airport lounge in Chicago.

Now a standard feature even among entry-level laptops, wireless Internet, or Wi-Fi, frees the computer user to work where and when they want, no longer constrained by a cord and an outlet to access the Internet at broadband speeds.

Whether they're used in a private space (such as a home or office) or commercial location (such as a coffee shop or airport), Wi-Fi enabled smartphones are capable of downloading data at much higher speeds, and at lower cost, than what your cell phone provider is offering. Wi-Fi is faster than most cellular data connections, even 3G, so bandwidth-intensive things such as Web browsing and downloads are much faster. Not only is Wi-Fi faster but also cheaper by avoiding cellular charges, thus you can save money with Wi-Fi.

PALM: The Early PDA

Regardless of how things go for this financially beleaguered company, Palm pioneered the modern personal digital assistant (PDA) that was a big part of the development of smartphones when combined with the capability of a cell phone.

In March 1996, less than three years after Apple's first Newton MessagePad attracted much media interest but little commercial success, Palm Computing (a division of U.S. Robotics) brought to market a pair of PDAs that offered some of the Newton's most interesting features (including the Graffiti handwriting-recognition system) without its hefty price tag or bulk.

In the early 2000s, successfully marrying a PDA to a cell phone, with data capabilities, became the Holy Grail of handheld computing. Several Palm licensees brought products to market, but their efforts were typically too large, too heavy, and insufficiently phone-like.

After several designs that quickly became outdated, the Palm Pre, released by Sprint in June 2009, is a late-game attempt to regain its former preeminence in the handheld universe. In 2010, Motorola introduced, with much fanfare and a massive TV ad campaign, Droid 2, said to be 40 percent faster than Motorola's original Droid.

BlackBerry Arrives

Some people believe BlackBerrys have become cult devices, inspiring a kind of slavish devotion perhaps matched only by Apple products. It's hard to imagine that early BlackBerry models didn't support voice calls, but it took Research In Motion Ltd. (RIM) a good four years or so to make a phone a standard feature of BlackBerry devices.

It's been 10 years since RIM rolled out the first BlackBerry device. In that decade, BlackBerry has become synonymous with mobility and is seen as the gold standard for mobile applications such as e-mail and calendaring.

BlackBerry is credited with creating some of the most forward-thinking, feature-packed smartphones out there—a huge transition from the clunky, brick-styled devices of yore. Today, you can't ride a train or grab a cup of coffee without seeing someone with their face aglow with the backlight from his or her BlackBerry screen as he or she scrolls through e-mails and messages.

The addictive nature of the devices has led some users to refer to them as "CrackBerrys" because of the drug-like hold they have on their loyal users.

The Big "Push"

BlackBerry didn't just make mobile e-mail useful, uniform, and readily accessible; it helped pioneer the very concept of "push." Push continues to be an elusive, contentious technology for users of many systems, devices, and mobile platforms to this day. Push technology enables you to receive a message instantly rather than waiting, and RIM was well ahead of the game here, touting its push technology by name as early as 2001. If someone sent you an e-mail, you had it immediately.

Meeting requests zipped down to you the second they were made. Of course, push ultimately went on to become one of the BlackBerry hallmarks and one of the major reasons users continue to steadfastly refuse to try other platforms. No matter how outdated RIM's timeworn interface may seem, by modern standards, it's a really powerful selling point.

As in the early days, the company is once again taking criticism for driving a theme into the ground. The other side of the argument, of course, is that they've settled on a winning formula, refining it year after year without messing with a very successful recipe.

Regardless of which side of the fence you are on, it is very much a matter of personal opinion, and in some ways it says something about one's personality. It's a choice between productivity and multimedia. A BlackBerry can be your music player just as an iPhone can connect to your Exchange account. It's ultimately a question of priorities and, for some, allegiances.

The Arrival of the iPhone

In fall 2006, almost a year after Steve Jobs had directed Apple's top engineers to create the iPhone, it was clear that the prototype was a disaster. It was full of bugs, and it didn't work. The phone dropped calls constantly, the battery stopped charging before it was full, and data and applications routinely became corrupted and unusable. The list of problems seemed endless.

For those working on the iPhone, the next three months would be the most stressful of their careers. Screaming matches broke out routinely in the hallways. Engineers, frazzled from all-night coding sessions, quit, only to rejoin days later after catching up on their sleep.

Six months later, on June 29, 2007, the iPhone went on sale. It is estimated to be the fastest-selling smartphone of all time and may well be Apple's most profitable device. As important as the iPhone has been to Apple and AT&T, its real impact is on the structure of the $11 billion-a-year U.S. mobile phone industry.

A Tipping Point for the Wireless Industry

This 4.8-ounce thin slice of glass and aluminum device was a change agent that would forever impact the mobile-phone business, taking power from carriers and giving it to manufacturers, developers, and consumers.

After a year and a half of secret meetings, Jobs had finally negotiated terms with the wireless division of the telecom giant AT&T (Cingular at the time) to be the iPhone's carrier. In return for five years of exclusivity, roughly 10 percent of iPhone sales in AT&T stores, and a thin slice of Apple's iTunes revenue, AT&T had granted Jobs unprecedented freedom and power.

He had convinced AT&T to spend millions of dollars and thousands of man-hours to create a new feature, so-called visual voice mail, and to reinvent the time-consuming in-store sign-up process. He'd also wrangled a unique revenue-sharing arrangement.

In addition, Apple retained complete control over the design, manufacturing, and marketing of the iPhone. Jobs had accomplished the unthinkable: He had squeezed a good deal out of one of the largest players in the well-established wireless industry.

Major Change in the Balance of Power

For decades, wireless carriers have treated manufacturers like serfs, using access to their networks as leverage to dictate what phones will get made, how much they will cost, and what features will be available on them. Handsets were viewed largely as cheap, disposable lures, massively subsidized to snare subscribers and lock them into using the carriers' proprietary services.

The iPhone upsets that balance of power. Carriers are learning that the right phone—even an expensive one—can win customers and bring in revenue. Now, in the pursuit of an Apple-like contract, every manufacturer is racing to create a phone that consumers will love, instead of one that carriers approved.

It may appear that the carriers' nightmares have been realized—that the iPhone has given all the power to consumers, developers, and manufacturers, while turning wireless networks into dumb pipes. But by fostering more innovation, carriers' networks could get more valuable, not less. Consumers will spend more time on devices, and thus on networks, racking up bigger bills and generating more revenue for everyone.

Apple's iPad

After months of speculation, Steve Jobs introduced the iPad in January 2010, which Apple hopes will be the coolest device on the planet. For all the hoopla surrounding it, however, the question is whether the iPad can achieve anything close to the success of the iPhone, which transformed the cell phone, forcing the industry to race to catch up.

Apple considers the device a pioneer in a new genre of computing, somewhere between a laptop and a smartphone. Some versions of the iPad can, for a monthly fee, use a 3G data connection like mobile phones, but the only carrier mentioned was AT&T. Apple says the iPad will run the 140,000 applications developed for the iPhone and the iPod Touch, but the company expects a new wave of programs tailored to the iPad.

With the success of the iPhone and its cousin, the iPod, it is likely that the iPad will follow a similar path. People have been willing to pay in order to customize those devices with applications, turning them into video game machines, compasses, city guides, and e-book readers.

Smartphone Applications

Smartphones, including iPhone and Blackberry, provide advanced features similar to the function of a PC. The smartphone operating system software provides a standardized user interface and platform for software applications.

Smartphones have advanced features such as e-mail, Internet, e-book reader ability, enhanced video camera, touch-screen keyboards. and much more. In short, smartphones are miniature computers that have phone capabilities but without the multitasking features.

The demand for these advanced mobile devices that boast powerful processors, abundant memory, large screens, and open operating systems has outpaced the rest of the mobile phone market and is anticipated to continue for years to come.

In the process of the development of new applications, cloud computing has emerged as an important computing technology that uses the Internet and central remote servers to maintain data and applications. It allows consumers and businesses to use applications without installation and provides access to their personal files with any computer on the Internet.

Conquering the Cloud...

Today, cloud computing is a fact of life if you use Gmail, Facebook, Flickr, Twitter, Google Buzz, or any of their contemporaries. Much of what makes you a unique individual is stored in some nebulous group network of servers you'll never see. These servers include numerous massive computers that look like overgrown refrigerators, sound like jet engines, and live in cold, windowless facilities close to power plants with astoundingly fast Internet connections.

In 2001, the cloud as we know it today was just an idea on a whiteboard (at the time, no one called it "the cloud") but BlackBerry customers were starting to taste some bits and pieces of the experience. RIM used CTIA Wireless in Vegas that year as the venue to introduce the next iteration of its connected experience: wireless calendar synchronization.

Up until this point, the BlackBerry platform had been about e-mails first and everything else second, and really, you could argue that's still the primary focus today. At the time, however, the company was starting to acknowledge that a businessperson's mobile office was about more than messaging and was beginning to act as a fast way to access PC-type features, such as checking on the schedule for the day, when it's not always convenient to pop open the laptop.

Is Broadband Spectrum a Choke Point?

As demand for smartphones explodes, it appears about the only thing that could put a crimp in growth would be a lack of broadband spectrum.

Wireless capacity, often an afterthought of smartphone buyers, is critical, because it's the ability to connect to the many apps and services that make consumers want a smartphone in the first place.

Factors such as weather, trees, network loads, cell tower locations, and other things can cause service from a single wireless service to vary widely from day to day and even from neighborhood to neighborhood, according to tests run by *PCWorld* magazine.

The recent advertising feud between AT&T and Verizon Communications raises the possibility that mobile broadband could become a choke point as more users stream video, read e-mail, and update their Twitter and Facebook pages on the go.

Industry research indicates that demand for wireless broadband has grown 5,000 times in the last three years. That growth is actually expected to accelerate rapidly in the coming years.

In the face of exploding data-service demand and scarce wireless spectrum, some companies, including AT&T and Verizon, have hinted they may begin to quietly begin rationing duration and speed of 3G connections to their heavy bandwith users.

Smartphone Advantages and Disadvantages

Smartphones offer rapid communications and numerous features that are popular with adults and children alike. The disadvantages of mobile phones are focused on usage at times when the individual should not be distracted. The most obvious is when driving but also includes attendance at meetings when the sound of an arriving message results in an immediate reaction by the owner to view the message.

Smartphones and other mobile devices have begun to dominate the life of many individuals and become addictive, for both adults and children, resulting in a withdrawal from personal interaction and a reliance on more technically based relationships.

People who are naturally very shy have latched on to the smartphone and the computer with increased usage of Twitter and Facebook. Previously they may have had only a few friends; now they can have hundreds of friends and don't have to meet someone in person.

Smartphones, like many consumer technology applications, have distinct advantages with the ability to communicate by voice, text, and even e-mail anytime and anywhere. This ability has made frequent human-to-human interaction possible across vast geographical areas.

Disadvantages include limited attention span to other activities and tasks while chatting incessantly on mobile phones, hazardous driving while conversing, and becoming a slave to the attractions of the wireless communication gadget.

A lot of the recent press has given new life to the driver distraction issue. Lawmakers have introduced new bills to ban texting, companies have outlawed distracted driving in corporate vehicles, and even President Obama issued an executive order aimed at reducing distracted driving by federal employees. There is a possible solution with a new phone app that recently became available.

New Driving-Related Apps!

There is a relatively new BlackBerry application called ZoomSafer that is essentially an information/communication manager for your mobile phone. The application will suppress incoming text and phone messages when it detects that you are moving faster than 10 mph.

ZoomSafer is essentially a firewall for unwanted communication while driving, including some unique features involving social components. The app will send an auto-reply notifying a caller or text sender that you are currently driving. ZoomSafer also contacts social networks and updates the user's status message to let others know that he or she is currently driving.

Although ZoomSafer does not completely eliminate distraction from driving, the user does have the option to receive messages, texts, or e-mails from close business or personal contacts. At this point ZoomSafer turns the phone into a hands-free communication device similar to Ford Sync.

Users can respond to the priority contact by navigating through an auditory menu using speech commands. Users can choose to either receive the call or send a voice message reply by e-mail.

ZoomSafer is available for free (however, the free version does not include the voice command features) and is readily available to anyone with a BlackBerry. The availability of the product makes it an exciting intervention for helping to reduce distracted driving.

Health Concerns

Although there are many conflicting studies on the negative health effects of incessant mobile phone usage, including male infertility, the effect of microwave radiation on the brain and irregular sleep patterns in teens, have emerged as some of the major health issues associated with mobile phones usage.

For those concerned about the increased usage of smartphones, the National Cancer Institute says "use of 'hands-free' wireless technology, such as Bluetooth, is increasing and may contribute to (a reduction) in cellular telephone exposures."

In addition, the U.S. Food and Drug Administration has suggested some steps that cellular telephone users can take: reserve the use of cellular telephones for shorter conversations, or for times when a landline phone is not available, and switch to a type of mobile phone with a hands-free device, such as Bluetooth, that will place more distance between the head of the user and the antenna, where there is the greatest risk of radiation.

What Is Bluetooth?

Bluetooth is a way to connect and transfer information between devices such as mobile phones, laptops and PCs, printers, digital cameras, and video game consoles using radio frequencies securely.

According to the official Bluetooth site, "Bluetooth wireless technology is a short-range communications technology intended to replace the cables connecting portable and/or fixed devices while maintaining high levels of security. The key features of Bluetooth technology are robustness, low power, and low cost. The Bluetooth specification defines a uniform structure for a wide range of devices to connect and communicate with each other." Bluetooth is popular because it's cheap, it's automatic, and it doesn't require myriad wires!

Dealing With E-Mail

E-mail is the single biggest challenge for most people and the biggest source of stress people face at work because of the volume of information people are expected to process each day. The flood of information comes from many sources—both corporate and personal e-mail.

In addition, it comes from many social and networking sites such as LinkedIn, Facebook, and Twitter, plus the forwarding of text messages from mobile phone and instant messaging services.

No doubt that many of us suffer from information overload: too many e-mails and too many demands coming at us from many places. The result is a much more difficult working environment.

Although e-mail is the main culprit, the mobile phone with numerous apps, instant messaging, and the open office architecture creates an environment conducive to distractions from the work we are being paid to perform.

With E-Mail Overload, Try to Control the Information Sources

There is no easy solution to this problem. In many ways, we are at the mercy of messages we receive from the people we work with, important customers, and our family. No matter how conscientious you are about organizing your work methods and activities, there will always be interruptions.

The first step is to catch up with your overdue e-mail communications. Set up an electronic organization that enables you to locate information and respond in a timely manner.

Decide on a time in the day when you are free to review and respond to less-urgent e-mail and CC messages that do not need immediate attention. It is easier if you put those messages in a folder to be reviewed at a later time.

If you send a lot of e-mails, you can expect to receive a lot of e-mails. Thus, if you want less e-mail, reduce the number of e-mails that you originate. Try to be more selective about the e-mails you send and what they contain. This will help reduce the volume of e-mails you receive.

If e-mail messages go beyond three levels (origination, reply, and reply), you might consider making a phone call or scheduling a short one-on-one meeting if something is very complex or requires a high degree of clarification.

Some companies have reduced the number of e-mails by creating a company-wide portal where information can be posted, allowing people to access it at their discretion instead of having to process every e-mail. As a result, the information is no longer being pushed to the recipient but is pulled by the reader at his or her convenience.

Spam Filters

Spam can be a big time-waster when you receive marketing and other material you don't want. Most companies have robust spam-filtering software to limit this type of e-mail. You can also purchase software for your PC that will limit this type of communication.

Some e-mail services have very strong spam filters to limit these types of e-mails. In most cases, you can specify the types of e-mail that you consider to be spam and they will be deleted at a specified time in the future.

The only problem is that sometimes e-mails you wish to see have been placed in the spam folder, so it pays to check this folder from time to time for missing e-mails.

Sign Up for Fewer Publications

Another way to cut down on the number of e-mails is by not signing up for publications with limited application to your work or personal interests. If you decide to sign for some material, use a different e-mail address for this type of information. Establish a separate e-mail address limited to your primary work or interests.

Don't forget cell phone spam. It is a good idea to register with the National Do Not Call registry as all cell phone numbers became public in February 2010. To prevent being called by numerous marketers and having to pay for the interruption, make a call from your mobile phone to (888) 382–1222, or use the Internet address *www.donotcall.gov.*

E-Mail Management Ideas

Following are some ideas that have been developed by companies to simplify the e-mail overload and may save you a headache, some time, and extra work:

- Make sure the subject matter is stated clearly. Indicate if it needs action or is information.
- Limit each Email to a single topic.
- Use paragraphs and proper grammar.
- Keep the sarcasm out to avoid misunderstandings.
- Compose better messages, with bullets and underlining to stress importance.
- When including a Web address, type the full address, including *www.*
- Avoid long e-mails. If supporting information is needed, attach a document.
- Don't respond to an e-mail if you are upset. Wait until you calm down.
- Always use the spell-check feature. It will save some embarrassment.
- If you are sending a long "for your information" e-mail, summarize the important points at the top, so the recipient does not have to read the entire message.
- If revising an existing e-mail document, make the changes in color so they are obvious.

Finally, there are only four things to do with email messages at work:

1. Do it now.
2. Delegate it to the proper person.
3. Designate it (for larger tasks) to be done at a specific time in your task list, and set a reminder to complete it when needed.
4. Discard it or file it. Get rid of it, if you don't need a copy, or file it if needed in the future.

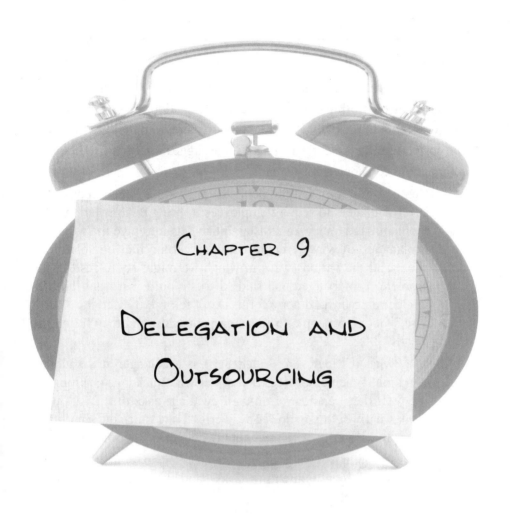

Chapter 9

Delegation and Outsourcing

"Getting results through people is a skill that
cannot be learned in the classroom."
—J. Paul Getty, American business executive

As I discussed in the Introduction, you are a limited resource. Even if you could somehow be productive every minute of your life, there are still only 24 hours in a day. You can't add a 25th. Or can you? Not to your own day, you can't. But you can get 25 or 50 or 75 hours worth of work done in a single day—or much more—by delegating or outsourcing some of your work to others. In fact, delegating or outsourcing is the only way to do this.

Practice the Art of Delegation

In *Time Power* (Harper & Row), Charles R. Hobbs defines delegation as "the act of controlling through others." Delegation, then, is more than just giving work to people; it's managing those people so they get that work done correctly and efficiently. Here are some suggestions that will help you be a more effective delegator/manager:

- ⏲ Demand solutions, not problems. Hobbs's key delegation principle is for managers to require employees to bring them solutions, not problems. Example: An assistant once began to give me a lengthy explanation of why we could not open certain files e-mailed by a client and the various ways in which we might try to resolve the problem. I interrupted and said, "I trust you. I just want the files in electronic or hard copy form. Don't tell me the details; I don't care." Get your people to focus on your ends, and they'll find the means.

- ⏲ Use "what if" logic. My sister, Fern, is a manager at a trade association. When employees bother her with questions or problems she feels they can answer on their own, she asks them, "If I were dead, what would you do?" Says Fern, "Nine times out of 10 they figure it out on their own without my help or further involvement."

- ⏲ Target productive work times. Managers who think their assistants will diligently attend to tasks handed to them at 3 p.m. on the Friday before a three-day weekend are fooling themselves. Assign involved tasks to employees when they are most likely to produce results. Fifty-one percent of 150 executives surveyed by Accountemps said Tuesday is the day of the week when employees are by far the most productive, reports *The Record* article "Dream Week For Bosses: Every Day is a Tuesday" (May 4, 1998). The worst day for productivity? Friday.

- ⏲ Add a human touch. The most valuable qualities you can develop within yourself are patience, kindness, and consideration for other people. Although machines and chemicals don't care whether you scream and curse at them, people do.

Your staff and coworkers are not just engineers, scientists, administrators, clerks, and programmers; they're people, first and foremost. They are people with families and friends, and likes and dislikes. People with feelings. Respect them as people, and you'll get their respect and loyalty in return. Treat them coldly and impersonally, and they will lose motivation to perform for you.

Corny as it sounds, the Golden Rule—"Do unto others as you would have others do unto you"—is a sound, proven management principle. The next time you're about to discipline a worker or voice your displeasure, ask yourself, "Would I like to be spoken to the way I'm thinking of speaking to him or her?" Give people the same kindness and consideration that you would want to receive if you were in their place.

Don't be overly critical. As a manager, it's part of your job to keep your people on the right track. That involves pointing out errors and telling them where they've gone wrong.

But some managers are overly critical. They're not happy unless they are criticizing. They rarely accomplish much or take on anything new themselves, but they are only too happy to tell others where they went wrong, why they're doing it incorrectly, and why they could do the job better. This takes up a lot of time in exchange for very little results.

Don't be this type of person. Chances are, you have more knowledge and experience in your field than a good many of the people you supervise. That's why the company made you the boss! Your job is to guide and teach these people—not to yell or nit-pick or show them how dumb they are compared to you.

Let them fail. Of course, to encourage people, you've got to let them make some mistakes.

Does this shock you? I'm not surprised. Most workers expect to be punished for every mistake. Most managers think it's a "black eye" on their record when an employee goofs. Successful managers know that the best way for their people to learn and grow is through experience and that means taking chances and making errors.

Give your people the chance to try new skills or tasks without a supervisor looking over their shoulders—but only on smaller, less crucial projects.

That way, mistakes won't hurt the company and can quickly and easily be corrected. On major projects, where performance is critical, you'll want to give as much supervision as is needed to ensure successful completion of the task.

What happens if an employee or subcontractor screws up really badly? "It ain't as bad you think it is," says Colin Powell. "It will look better in the morning. Get mad, then get over it."

Be available. Have you ever been enthusiastic about a project, only to find yourself stuck and unable to continue, while you waited for someone higher up to check your work before giving the go ahead for the next phase?

Few things dampen employee motivation and slow things down more than management inattention. As a manager, you have a million things to worry about besides the report sitting in your mailbox waiting for your approval. To the person who wrote that report, though, each day's delay causes frustration, anger, worry, and insecurity.

So although you've got a lot to do, give your first attention to approving, reviewing, and okaying projects in progress. If employees stop by to ask a question or discuss a project, invite him or her to sit down for a few minutes. If you're pressed for time, set up an appointment for later on that day and keep it. This will let your people know you are genuinely interested in them, and that's something they'll really appreciate.

Improve the work environment. People are most productive when they have the right tools and work in pleasant, comfortable surroundings.

Be aware that you may not be the best judge of what your employees need to do their jobs effectively. Even if you've done the job yourself, someone else may work best with a different set of tools, or in a different set-up, because each person is different.

If your people complain about work conditions, listen. These complaints are usually not made for selfish reasons but stem from each worker's desire to do the best job possible. By providing the right equipment or workspace, you can achieve enormous increases in output—often with a minimal investment.

Show interest in their lives. You can benefit by showing a little personal interest in your people: their problems, family life, health, and hobbies. This doesn't have to be insincere or overdone. It can simply be the type of routine conversation that should naturally pass between people who work closely.

Have you been ignoring your employees? Get into the habit of taking a few minutes every week (or every day) to say "hello" and chat for a minute or two. If an employee has a personal problem affecting his mood or performance, try to find out what it is and how you might help. Send a card or small gift on important occasions and holidays, such as a 10th anniversary with the firm or a birthday. Often, it is the little things we do for people (such as letting workers with long commutes leave early on a snowy day, or springing for dinner when overtime is required) that determine their loyalty to you.

Be open to ideas. You may think the sign of a good manager is to have a department where everybody is busy at work on their assigned tasks. If your people are merely "doing their jobs," they're only working at about half their potential. A truly productive department is one in which every employee is actively thinking of better, more efficient methods of working—ways in which to produce a higher-quality product, in less time, at lower cost.

To get this kind of innovation from your people, you have to be receptive to new ideas. What's more, you have to encourage your people to produce new ideas. Incentives are one way to motivate employees to be more productive. You can offer a cash bonus, time off, or a gift, but a more potent form of motivation is simply the employee's knowledge that management does listen to him or her, and does put employee suggestions and ideas to work.

When you listen to new ideas, be open-minded. Don't shoot down a suggestion before you've heard it in full. Many of us are too quick, too eager, to show off our own experience and knowledge, and say that something won't work because "we've tried it before" or "we don't do it that way." Well, maybe you did try it before, but that doesn't mean it won't work now. Having done things a certain way in the past doesn't mean you've necessarily been doing them the best way. A good manager is open-minded and receptive to new ideas.

Give your people room to advance. If a worker doesn't have a place to go, a position to aspire to, or a promotion to work toward, then the position is a dead-end job. Dead-end workers are usually bored, unhappy, and unproductive.

Organize your department so that everyone has opportunity for advancement—so that there is a logical progression up the ladder in terms of title, responsibility, status, and pay. If this isn't possible because your department is too small, perhaps that progression must inevitably lead to jobs outside the department. If so, don't hold people back; instead, encourage them to aim for these goals so that they will put forth their best efforts during all the years they are with you.

Delegate whatever you can. "Many things can be delegated to people who will not do them the way you would, won't do them as perfectly as you would, but will wind up with the same result," writes Dan Kennedy in *No B.S. Time Management for Entrepreneurs* (Self Counsel Press). "Every one of these things should be delegated."

Giving others work makes them more engaged in their jobs and saves you time. In *Workaholics,* Marilyn Machlowitz quotes psychotherapist Maryanne Vandervelde: "If you never have to cook your own dinner, take your own shirts to the laundry, arrange social engagements, worry about the details of a move, or stay home with a sick child, you can work harder, longer, and more efficiently."

Professionals who delegate are basically selling their time to an employer or a client, yet many office workers fritter their valuable time away handling the most mundane tasks. A better strategy is having employees or subcontractors do non-critical tasks for you.

Reward productive behavior. As management consultant Michael LeBouf notes, "The things that get rewarded get done." If you want people to get more done, create incentives for them to do that. One of the most popular incentives is "comp days" (days off given in return for extraordinary efforts during crunch periods).

The art of delegating is one that improves with practice. The more often you let other people help you get work done, the more often you'll see the positive results. You will have more time to do the things that only you can do, and you'll be getting much more than 24-hours worth of work done each and every day.

Get With It: Outsource

"All well and good for the corporate manager," some of you are now saying, "but I don't have employees, so I can't delegate."

Wrong. We all delegate every day. Every one of us. For example, instead of pressing our own pants, we tell the dry cleaner to do it. Instead of cleaning up the kids' toys, we tell the kids to tidy up after themselves.

Those who don't have employees still delegate. We delegate to vendors: service firms, freelancers, independent professionals, independent contractors, and others who will do what we tell them, for a fee rather than a salary. The practice of delegating work to vendors instead of staff employees is called outsourcing, and its popularity has grown tremendously in recent years.

According to a 2009 report by AMR Research, approximately 80 percent of enterprises plan to increase their amount of IT outsourcing or at least keep it the same. Offshore outsourcing is a $50 billion per year business. A University of California at Berkeley study warns that as many as 14 million Americans hold jobs at risk of being outsourced.

Why don't some companies outsource more? Some people hesitate for the following reasons:

- ⊕ They think they're too small to need help.
- ⊕ They don't have enough work to keep an assistant busy.
- ⊕ They don't make enough money to be able to afford to pay someone else to do some of their work.

As you become busier, you realize the amount of work you can do (and therefore the amount of income you can generate) is limited by your own energy and the number of hours you can work in a day. One way around this is to spend more of your time on billable work, especially work that earns a high hourly rate. To do this, you have to free up some time by not doing work that is not billable or work that is billed at a low rate. This is where hiring outside help comes in.

You make money by thinking and producing. Everything else—learning how to use a particular computer program, scanning source materials, going to the library, buying supplies—is a waste of time that could be spent on productive work. Some or all of these nonessential activities can easily be outsourced to others.

What should you outsource? Businesspeople outsource all different kinds of tasks, including:

- Research.
- Filing.
- Typing and word processing.
- Mailing list and database management.
- Telephone selling and telemarketing.
- Customer service.
- Proofreading.
- Sales and marketing.
- Bookkeeping and accounting.
- Computer programming.

You can outsource all of these or some of these tasks. It's up to you. My policy is to do all the high-end work myself and outsource the administrative, clerical, and secretarial work to subcontractors (which I'll discuss later).

Obviously, to make a profit, you have to pay the subcontractor less money than it would cost you to do the work yourself. This means either the subcontractors charge less per hour for their services than you do—or they charge less for the task because, given their high degree of proficiency, they can do it in a much shorter time frame than you can.

For example, I don't do my own filing, because I can pay someone to do it for me. It costs a fraction of the money I'd make spending the time on my writing and consulting projects. My attorney is more expensive and earns fees equivalent to mine, but I still use him on contracts and for other needs. Not only does he do a much better job than I would, but he can do in one hour (and bill me for one hour) what would take me half a day or more.

Outsourcing vs. Adding Staff

Let's say you are interested in getting more help around your office. A major decision is whether to hire an employee or outsource.

When you hire employees, they generally work on your premises using your office space, equipment, and supplies. You pay them a salary and often provide benefits such as sick days, vacation, and health insurance.

When you outsource, you contract with an individual or small firm that provides the services you need on a fee basis. This fee can be a project fee but is usually an hourly fee. Independent contractors typically work on their premises, using their office space, equipment, and supplies. You pay their invoice like you would pay a bill for any product or service you buy.

I have had both staff employees and subcontractors, and prefer the latter to the former by a wide margin. Here's why:

1. Subcontractors and other outsourced workers can perform as well as full-time employees but earn less. More often than not, they do not get a pension or healthcare benefits, so they are cheaper to employ.

2. There is no long-term commitment and no recurring overhead. You pay subcontractors only when you give them work to do. Employees get paid as long as they show up, whether they have work to do or not. When you don't need subcontractors, they work for their other clients (or take time off), and you don't pay them.

3. Subcontractors are independent and responsible for their own welfare. Employees may depend on you for guidance, career satisfaction, and other needs—a responsibility you may not want to deal with.

4. Using subcontractors is less complex, from an accounting and paperwork point of view, than having employees. Employees require social security tax, FICA, worker's compensation, and other complexities. Independent contractors are paid as vendors. Note: The Internal Revenue Service requires that people who are paid as independent contractors work on their premises and have other clients. Consult your accountant or tax attorney.

5. Subcontractors are more motivated because they are sellers and you are the buyer. They have a customer-service orientation, which is a welcome change from the attitude of resentment or indifference many employees seem to have toward the boss.

6. Subcontractors provide their own equipment and office space, buy their own furniture, and pay their own utility bills. Often the sub-contractor will have better equipment than you do, and, as their client, you get the benefit of this equipment without buying it.

Subcontracting can actually reduce your overhead and capital costs. Hiring employees increases it because you have to supply them with a fully equipped work space.

"Outsource everything other than your core function," recommends Stephen M. Polland in an article in Dan Kennedy's No B.S. Marketing Letter newsletter. His advice includes replacing full- and part-time staff-ers with independent contractors or other entrepreneurs, leasing or renting rather than owning hard assets, and focusing on personal productivity and profitability.

Where to Find Help Through Outsourcing

When my longtime staff assistant quit to take another job, I wondered where I would find another assistant. A colleague suggested that, instead of hiring a full-time assistant, I could find a typing/word processing/adminis-trative service to handle my needs.

I looked in the local paper and yellow pages and called several services. I explained that I was a busy writer looking for substantial administrative support and asked each service—most of whom were individuals working from their homes—whether they would be interested in having a client who would provide them a substantial amount of business on a regular basis.

Every service I talked to was excited at the prospect of having such a client! Apparently, the word-processing and typing business is sporadic and project-oriented; having a regular client on retainer was unusual and a wel-come change that would bring greater income and financial security.

I interviewed several word-processing services and chose one person. I explained that I would buy 30 hours of her time a week, by the week, and pay for a month's worth of service in advance at the beginning of each month. In return, I wanted the best rate she could offer me and a high level of service.

This person, who is now my assistant, works for me from her home in a town 8 miles away. It's close enough that she can easily come over to do some work here or pick up materials if required, but most often we work by phone, fax, and e-mail. In fact, her small word-processing business has a part-time messenger to serve me and her other clients, and I see her only a few times a year.

This "virtual office" approach has many advantages and few drawbacks. In addition to the advantages of outsourcing already discussed, I can work in privacy without having my assistant physically present (privacy and solitude are, to me, prime productivity boosters).

The only drawback is that my subcontractor isn't here all of the time to run certain errands, but I found a solution: I hired my former secretary as a second subcontractor. She works for me after her regular job, from 4:30 p.m. to 7:30 p.m. and can therefore go to the post office and bank, and do other errands. I also have an independent sales rep who negotiates deals for me with corporate clients, a literary agent who does the same with publishers, an accountant who does my taxes, and a freelance bookkeeper who handles accounts payable and receivable. Obviously, I am a big fan of outsourcing. It works for me and I recommend that you try it.

I found my sales rep when I went to a trade show and attended a workshop on self-promotion for freelancers. I was so impressed that I called the presenter after the seminar and asked if she would represent me so that I could outsource all of my personal selling to her. She agreed, and it has worked beautifully ever since. She is compensated similarly to the way literary agents are compensated (based on a percentage of my gross sales).

Start small. Hire a part-time assistant or word processor to work for you one day a week. If you can keep this person busy, and if you like having the help and feel it frees you to increase your output and income, you can always buy more of the person's time or, if he or she is too busy, hire a second helper.

One caveat: Because many of your colleagues may not use subcontractors, you may not be able to find someone through referral. Call people who advertise word processing, typing, or secretarial assistance in the local town paper and Yellow Pages. Meet with them face to face for an interview before hiring them. Start on a trial basis, and don't promise anything more regular until both of you are satisfied the relationship is working well.

You might also consider using college students who can be hired as part-time assistants or summer interns. The problem is that after the summer, or when they graduate, they're gone. The value of an assistant increases as that person learns your procedures and business over time; this advantage does not exist when you hire college students and other transients who don't stick around. A professional word processor or assistant running his or her own service business, on the other hand, wants to make that business grow and is looking for long-term client relationships. That's why I prefer to outsource to professionals rather than to students.

The Value of Delegating and Outsourcing

Look around you. Everywhere within a one-hour drive are co-workers, colleagues, suppliers, vendors, retailers, service firms, and other resources that are ready and willing to do the work you want to avoid. They'll iron your clothes, clean your apartment, or even wash your hair for you!

My uncle Ira, a successful entrepreneur, taught me the lesson of valuing one's time and not wasting it on trivial tasks. When I moved from Baltimore to New York City to take a job, Ira asked me, "Are you eating balanced meals?"

No, I replied. I had a tiny kitchen and a pint-sized refrigerator in my cramped Manhattan apartment. I ate pizza, subs, Chinese food, and other take-out. My mother had promised to give me some recipes for healthy meals, which I intended to cook.

"Don't waste your time," said Uncle Ira wisely. "Go to the coffee shop or diner on your block. For five or six bucks plus tip, you'll get a meal including soup, salad, beverage, meat or chicken or turkey, potato, and vegetable. They'll cook it for you, serve it to you, take away the dishes—and it will cost about the same as making it yourself."

Though I still prefer to eat at home rather than in restaurants, I understood and began practicing the principle: Your time has value. Don't waste it. If you can buy a thing at less cost than the value of your time to do it yourself, buy it.

I agree with the philosophy of "make or buy" described by consultant Richard V. Benson in his *Secrets of Successful Direct Mail* (NTC Business Books): "Make only that to which you bring a unique quality and buy everything else around the corner." I hope I bring a unique value to the books and copy I write for my publishers and clients. I know I don't bring it to a turkey dinner.

Polish Those People Skills

We all know people with great "people skills" and sometimes wonder, "How do they do it?" It's simply a matter of knowing the basics of how to deal with other people and then making a conscious effort to put those basics into practice. Here are seven habits of businesspeople who know how to get the most out of the vendors they delegate or outsource to:

1. They present their best selves to the public. Your moods change but your vendors, customers, and colleagues don't care. Make a conscious effort to be your most positive, enthusiastic, helpful self, especially when that's not how you feel. If you need to vent, do it in private.

2. They answer phone calls promptly. Few things annoy people more than not having their phone calls returned. Get back to people within two hours. If you can't, have your voice mail guide them to others who can help. If you're really uncomfortable with certain people and don't want to talk with them on the phone, answer their query through a fax or e-mail, or call when you know they won't be there and leave a message on their voice mail.

3. They call people by their names and ask questions about their lives. Take the time to learn and use everyone's name, especially assistants. Most people don't. You don't have to glad-hand everyone, but if you see a child's picture on someone's desk, he or she would probably appreciate your asking, "How old is your daughter?" Establishing some common bond makes the other person more receptive to working with you.

4. They meet people halfway. Sometimes we're right and the other person is wrong, but many people I observe seem to enjoy going out of their way to rub this fact in the other person's face. Give instructions, corrections, and criticisms without making the other person feel stupid or ignorant (such as, "That's a good idea, but given the process variables, here's another approach we should also consider.").

5. They listen carefully before speaking. A sure sign you are not listening to the other person is that you can't wait to say what you want to say. As soon as the other person pauses, you jump in and start talking. Even if you think you know how the story ends, listen to the other person. This person's knowledge and grasp of the situation may surprise you. If not, listening shows you considered his or her opinion and didn't just steamroll over the thought.

6. They maintain eye contact. When you're talking with someone, look him or her in the eye at points in the conversation. If you're explaining something while typing on a keyboard, take your eyes away from the screen now and then to look and talk directly at the other person.

7. They are not afraid to admit when they are wrong. People are afraid that other people will think they are incompetent if they admit to being wrong. The opposite is true. Andrew Lanyi, a stock market expert, explains, "The more you are willing to admit that you are not a guru, the more credibility you gain." No one knows everything, and everybody knows people make mistakes. If you refuse to admit your mistakes or if you pretend to know everything, people won't trust you when you are right and do know the answer.

Although they will never admit it, vendors have favorite and least-favorite clients. The rating you get as a client depends, in large part, on how well you treat the vendor as a business colleague and a human being. Despite claims that "every client is important," favorite clients often get preferential treatment; unpopular clients frequently go to the bottom of the priority list.

Poor communication is yet another barrier to working effectively with the people you delegate or outsource work to. Here are steps you can take to get your message across so everyone understands and no one is frustrated by the communication process:

- Listen and make sure you understand. Listening is a skill that requires your full attention. Don't have a conversation while you're checking your e-mail or searching Websites. Do one thing at a time and you will do each thing well.

- Prove you understand—feed it back. When another person asks you a question or makes a statement, repeat it back in your own words and ask whether that's what the person meant. Very often, what he or she said—or what you heard—is not exactly what the person was trying to get across, and the two of you need to try again.

- Never underestimate the intelligence of the average person. People who don't know your company, products, or technology may simply lack the technical background, data, and aptitude—and not intelligence. Explain technical concepts in plain, simple language. Avoid jargon or at least define technical terms before using them. A "fractional T1 circuit" may confuse your boss, client, or electrician, but everyone understands the concept of a "telephone line."

- Talk to people at their level, not yours. In addition to keeping things simple, focus on what's important to the other person, which is not necessarily what is important to you. For example, a graphic designer I know goes into elaborate explanations of kerning and fonts when all I want to know is whether to make the headline bigger.

- Make sure they get it. People often don't ask questions for fear of being perceived as stupid. Encourage listeners to stop you and ask questions if they don't understand. Ask them questions so you know whether they got it. If not, find out what they don't understand. Then make it clear to them.

- Don't assume. The old joke goes, "When you assume, you make an 'ass' of 'u' and 'me.'" If you want someone to run a simulation on Windows Vista, for example, make sure he or she Windows Vista installed on his or her PC and knows how to use it.

- Don't let your annoyance and impatience show. Sure, it can be frustrating explaining what, to you, are familiar topics, especially to people who don't have the background. If you act annoyed, lose your patience, or become arrogant, your listener will be turned off—and you'll make an enemy instead of an ally.

⊕ Budget communications time into the schedule. Part of the frustration people feel explaining projects, policies, and objectives is the time it takes, which they could be spending on their "real" work. The solution is to accept that communication is a mandatory requirement on every project and budget communications time into your schedule accordingly.

⊕ Use the 80/20 rule. The most effective communicators spend 80 percent of their time listening and only 20 percent talking. Many of us like to lecture, pontificate, or explain details of no interest to the other person. Instead, let the other people tell you what they need and want, and then give it to them. When you waste a person's time, your relationship becomes less profitable—and they can quickly lose enthusiasm.

⊕ Make a friend. If there is chemistry or camaraderie between you and the vendor, let your relationship flow and grow naturally. You shouldn't force a connection where there is none, and you don't have to be a social butterfly when you're not. But as a rule, people prefer to deal with people they like. Make it easy for the other person to like you, or at least don't give them reasons to dislike you.

Here are some additional tips to improve your ability to deal effectively with other people:

⊕ Prefer positive to negative statements. Instead of "George didn't finish coding the system," say, "George got 95 percent of the coding done." Instead of saying something is bad, say it's good but could be made even better. Instead of saying someone "failed" to do something, just say he didn't do it.

⊕ Don't speak when you're angry. Cool off. Don't feel you have to answer a criticism or complaint on the spot. Instead say, "Let me give it some thought and get back to you. Is tomorrow morning good?" This prevents you from saying things you'll regret later or making snap decisions.

⊕ Don't use value judgments to make people feel bad about mistakes. Avoid the implication that errors in judgment, which are temporary and one-time, are due to character and intelligence flaws. Don't say, "That was stupid"; instead say, "We can't ever let that happen again." Focus on preventing future repetitions of the mistake rather than assigning blame.

- Be courteous but don't overdo humility. Be pleasant and personable, but avoid fawning. Treat other people with respect and insist they do the same with you in return. For example, if a person is clearly technology-phobic, don't falsely flatter that person with malarkey about how quickly they're catching on—unless they really are.

- Empathize before stating an opinion. Don't seek out an argument; argue only when necessary. Make the conversation collaborative rather than adversarial. Say, "I understand" when the other person gives his or her opinion. "I understand" doesn't mean you agree; it means you heard what that person said and considered it in forming your own opinion, which you're now going to present.

- Apologize completely. Apologies should be unconditional: "I was wrong," not "I know I did X but that's because you did Y." Don't try to bring third parties or external factors into the equation. The bottom line is: It was your responsibility. Admit your mistakes and move on.

Use Long-Distance Delegation and Outsourcing

In today's global society, many of us deal with colleagues and suppliers who might be across the country or even around the world. We can still offload tasks to them, but managing the long-distance relationship has some added challenges, especially when different languages, cultures, and time zones are involved.

In an article in *Quality First* newsletter, business writer Marilyn Pincus gives the following five tips for working effectively with long-distance coworkers and vendors:

1. Distant coworkers are like customers. Do your best to serve them.

2. Try to personalize some of your conversations with distant coworkers. This helps establish a friendly environment. "When individuals feel kindly toward one another, there's a natural tendency to cooperate," says Pincus.

3. Listen carefully. Make sure everyone understands who is to do what and when.

4. Notify distant coworkers immediately of any delays or complications.

5. Identify expectations. For instance, if you're only available during normal business hours, distant workers may be required to take phone calls from you early in the morning or late at night, and possibly at home. Are they willing?

Do you feel you have to do everything yourself? Then you will never get everything done. Only by delegating or outsourcing to others can you go beyond your own limited personal effort and energy and make the most of every second of every day.

Chapter 10

Getting Organized

"Life is tough; it takes a lot of your time."
—Sean Morey, comedienne

If you don't think it's necessary to be organized in order to use time efficiently, think again. The average adult spends 16 hours a year searching for misplaced keys, according to *Reader's Digest*. An article in *Business Marketing* reports that, according to an Internet survey of executives, being disorganized wastes at least an hour a day. At the end of a year, that's an awful lot of wasted time!

Getting organized does require effort, but the long-term rewards far exceed the short-term costs. People have asked me, "Doesn't it take a lot of time to go through all your to-do lists and systems each day?" I answer, "A lot less time than if I didn't have these systems and was less organized!"

On the other hand, the fear that time-management technology may be too complex is well-founded. Some time-management systems and products do take more time than they save.

The key is simplicity. My advice: Use what works for you, and discard the rest. If a method is not comfortable or a tool is too complex, find something else.

A 1999 study by the Merck Family Fund found that 62 percent of surveyed adults agreed with the statement "I would like to simplify my life." Yet most people don't make even the tiniest effort toward making their lives simpler. Even when they view not having enough time as the number-one or number-two problem in their lives, they spend zero time and effort seeking to remedy the situation. They continue their disorganized ways and refuse to change, which of course means the condition of not having enough time will not change either.

Get It Together

"Organization is the key to moving forward in life or in business," says professional organizer Sandee Corshen in an article in *American Way.* "You can't deal with today if yesterday is staring you in the face."

Disorganized people are inefficient, because they have to expend extra time and effort—calling the bank to get a duplicate copy of a statement already received and now lost, running to the crowded mall at the last minute to buy a forgotten holiday present, standing in line at the post office on April 14th waiting to mail income tax returns. All of these activities waste time because of poor organizational and planning skills.

Here are some techniques that can help you organize your life and save time both at work and at home:

- ⏱ Carry a pocket to-do list and a pen, or personal digital assistant (PDA), at all times. Write down thoughts and ideas as they occur. Just as a computer's random access memory is erased when the power goes out, our brains lose track of thoughts, ideas, plans, and tasks as we tire or take on too much new information. Carry a pad and pen so you can jot reminders, notes, ideas, and priority items as you think of them. I always wear shirts with breast pockets so I can carry my pad and pen. It takes no work for the paper to remember them, but it exhausts your brain to do so. Why take the chance of having the day's priorities fade from your awareness? Write it down.

- ⏱ Write down thoughts and ideas as soon as they occur. The key to superior achievement is not having ideas—everyone has loads of them—but implementing them. You can't implement an idea if you don't remember it and make it an action item. You won't remember your ideas unless you write them down as soon as they occur. If you wait even an hour, you'll forget—and never record—more than 90 percent of the ideas you have. Again, most people don't have a shortage of ideas, but they do have too-short idea lists—because they don't write things down.

- ⏱ Create filing systems for every aspect of your life. To be truly well-organized, you have to create a specific place for all information and ideas. The best way to do this is to have a well-organized filing system covering every aspect of your life, not just major work projects. For instance, have you ever had an appliance break down that you thought might be covered by warranty, only to discover that you have no idea where the receipt and warranty are? The solution I use is to keep warranties, receipts, and instruction manuals for all household appliances and consumer electronics in a big three-ring binder labeled "HOME." Also included in the notebook are bills and guarantees for major home repairs, such as our new roof and added family room.

The advantage of such a system is that I can quickly retrieve the papers I need without a time-consuming search. It also eliminates the problem of lost documents. With the document quickly in hand, we can easily and inexpensively take care of household problems either by troubleshooting them on our own (following the instructions we've saved) or by taking advantage of manufacturers' warranties that are still in force. This saves a considerable amount of time and money.

⊕ Don't be a pack-rat. Clutter is the enemy of efficiency. To reduce clutter, periodically purge your file cabinets, hard disk drive, and bookshelves of old material you no longer need. Rule of thumb: If you haven't looked at it in a year or more you can probably throw it out. (Exceptions: bank statements, W-2 forms, and other financial records. These should be kept for seven years.)

⊕ Keep a calendar of appointments and deadlines. In Chapter 1, I stressed the advantages of posting to-do lists on a wall near you so they are always visible. "Out of sight, out of mind" is an old saying and a true one. If something isn't in front of your eyes, it tends to get tucked away in the back of your mind.

Professionals with busy schedules and multiple tasks may want to use a more sophisticated system than my simple wall-mounted 8 ½ x 11 inch to-do lists. "Visual organizers" can solve the problem. A visual organizer is a wall-mounted system for prominent visual display of a continually updated calendar, schedule, task, or to-do list. Most visual organizers are made of a piece of laminated plastic that can be mounted on a wall and written on with colored dry-erase markers. The writing can be erased with a paper towel or eraser, making it easy to add updates and corrections to the schedule as needed.

⊕ Cork a wall. A bulletin board is another tool that helps you stay organized by putting tasks, papers, memos, lists, business cards, project schedules, policies, procedures, and other priority items in constant view.

If you use a bulletin board but find you run out of space too easily, consider affixing cork panels to all or part of a wall in your office. The cork wall gives you a convenient, easy, highly visible system for organizing and displaying work materials.

Cubicle workers often complain about being in cubicles, but one advantage of cubicles is that the walls are covered with soft material into which pushpins can easily be inserted. Therefore, if you're in a cubicle, every vertical surface can be used as a bulletin board.

⊕ Keep a clean desk. In the movie *How to Succeed in Business Without Really Trying,* Robert Morse convinces his boss that he is a hard worker by littering his desk with papers, coffee cups, and cigarettes to give the appearance of busyness. It works—in the movie. But reality is something else: According to an article in *The Record* (January 18, 1999), the average executive loses six weeks a year retrieving misplaced information from messy desks and missing files.

A messy desk is also an impediment to productivity. It limits your actual workspace because only a small fraction of the desk surface can be used for your current project; the rest is tied up as a storage medium. You can't fully concentrate on the current task because the other papers staring in your face distract you by serving as a constant reminder of other pressures and work to be done.

⊕ Put things in the same place every time. I mentioned at the beginning of this chapter that the average adult spends 16 hours a year searching for lost keys. This won't happen if you put things in the same place every time. This organizational tip goes for all aspects of your life: business projects, financial documents, pictures, mementos, keys, medical records, receipts, warranties, gloves, mittens, raincoats, boots, lunch boxes, tools. Keep each item in the same place all the time. If you get into this habit, remembering where things are becomes automatic, and the items will always be there when you look. Until then, keep a master list of common items and their locations as a memory aid.

⊕ Keep things in their appropriate space. Clutter is the enemy of organization and productivity. Clutter occurs when materials, equipment, and tools for one task or area spill out into another area. Home-based workers frequently tell me that their home offices, intended to be confined to a spare bedroom or finished basement, have spilled out into other living areas such as the dining room or kitchen table.

Put everything in its appropriate place. Use storage racks, stackable boxes, shelving, and whatever else helps you organize your possessions. Kids' toys stay in the toy box, newspapers for recycling stay in the pantry, and so on. If the pantry is full with papers, you have to take them to the recycling center and not let them spill into the kitchen.

Stop to Take a Pulse

Frank Bettger, in his best-selling book, *How I Raised Myself From Failure to Success in Selling* (Prentice Hall), comments:

One of the greatest satisfactions in life comes from getting things done and knowing you have done them to the best of your ability. If you are having trouble getting yourself organized, if you want to increase your ability to think, and do things in the order of their importance, remember there is only one way: Take more time to think and do things in the order of their importance.

Set aside one day as a self-organization day, or a definite period each week. The whole secret of freedom from anxiety over not having enough time lies not in working more hours but in the proper planning of hours.

"I dedicate one afternoon or evening a week to doing nothing but relaxing at home," said technical writer Amy Shogan in an interview with *Intercom* magazine. "The catch is, while I 'relax' I tie up all the loose ends that we don't usually find time to do during the week." For Shogan, this includes sorting through mail, paying bills, returning calls, writing out a list of to-dos, reading, and planning for the following week. In the same article, Nancy Coleman, also a technical writer, advises drawing up the next day's to-do list at the end of each day. The list, says Nancy, should include the top three to five things that must be done immediately.

These strategies will all help you keep a finger on the pulse of your professional and personal life so you never have to waste time wandering around wondering what to do next.

Organize, Store, and Retrieve Critical Data

Irrelevant information is a great time-waster, but relevant information that is not organized properly can also steal away precious hours of work time from a very busy schedule. Organizing information wisely increases its value to you; sloppy information organization decreases its utility.

The computer gives us an enormous advantage in managing information assets: Information converted to computer-file format is much more easily manipulated, stored, retrieved, transmitted, and used than paper files.

If you are a professional working primarily with information, your computer files are perhaps your most valuable asset. Efficient use of them can save you time and effort while making you more productive. Poor computer-file management can cause you to waste hours searching for data and recreating documents and images that already exist (but that you can't find).

Therefore, you should practice good digital-file management techniques. Digital files need to be organized in a sensible fashion and labeled in such a way that they can quickly and easily be retrieved, by a variety of selection criteria (keyword, topic, project, customer, version, content, date) when needed.

In an interview with *Publishing & Production Executive* magazine, Neil O'Callaghan, vice president of Applied Graphics Technology in New York City, defines digital asset management as "a system and its associated workflow processes which facilitate the organization of digital media files—images, logos, graphics, pages, text, fonts, video, audio, and so forth—in such a manner as to allow for easy querying, asset information retrieval, asset identification, asset conversion, and export into a myriad of applications."

Even minor technology features can greatly enhance digital asset management. Two examples are Windows XP and bookmarks. In DOS and Windows 3.1, computer files were limited to eight characters, resulting in all sorts of arcane file names in a creative effort to make them memorable and retrievable—which usually failed. Windows 95 and higher permit much longer file names, so file names can be more specific and descriptive, and thus easier to find and retrieve.

Another valuable tool is the bookmark feature included on most Web browsers. When you find a Website you'll reference frequently or even occasionally, you can use the bookmark feature to add it to a list of favorite Websites. These are stored in the browser for future reference, and are available whenever you access the Web. This prevents you from forgetting key Website addresses and having to search for sites you've already visited.

If you have a lot of files on a particular topic, project, or customer, maintain an index of them as a separate file. For instance, if the customer is General Motors, make all the files begin with GM; that way, they are all grouped together on your directory—without the need to create a subdirectory. The index file would be called "GMINDEX." In it would be a list of all file names, followed by a brief description. Therefore, "GMPR1" would be press release number one about the GM account.

Here are some tips for organizing your electronic files more efficiently:

- Keep a set of "boilerplate" files. These are pieces of text, graphics, drawings, routine correspondence, and presentations you've created for one job that you can reuse in other jobs. If you write sales proposals, for example, one boilerplate file might be your company's corporate bio that appears at the end of each proposal. If you write field inspection reports, much of the language might be similar or even exactly the same from one inspection to the next. Why reinvent the wheel each time? Name these files and keep a master list of them so you can find them easily when you need them.

- Keep a directory that enables you to locate boilerplate documents quickly by topic. It doesn't do any good to have a great boilerplate paragraph on disk when finding it takes more time than rewriting it from scratch.

- Get a scanner. Many times, you'll be incorporating into your own work sentences and paragraphs from other documents created by other people (being careful not to plagiarize, of course). You will have hard copies of these documents but not the electronic files. It's a waste of time to key these documents into your computer by hand. Scanning saves a lot of time. You can buy a decent scanner today for less than $200.

- Use logical filenames—"JSMEM1," for example, for memo number one to John Smith, or "OUTREP1" for a report on outsourcing.

- Always type the file name at the top of page one of the document, as follows: "filename: OUTREP1." Often you come across a hard copy of something you've written in a file folder, and want to find the electronic file so you don't have to rekey it. Putting the name of every file on the first page of the document makes it easy to find the electronic files. If you can't, you have to scan or retype the material, which is boring as well as a waste of your time.

⊕ Store any document you might reuse in whole or in part on your hard drive. Make sure your PC has at least several gigabytes of hard disk storage to accommodate a large number of stored documents. When evaluating whether to add a document to your collection, the rule of thumb is this: When in doubt, don't throw it out.

Organize Your Paper Overload

Not all the information you need will be stored on a computer. There will always be paper files that need to be organized in some recognizable manner before you find yourself squished into a corner of a room overflowing with boxes and file folders. According to Stephanie Denton, a professional organizer, in an article in *Men's Health,* the average U.S. executive spends the equivalent of six weeks a year searching for misplaced information. There's got to be a better way.

"Practice good filing 'hygiene,'" advises my colleague Jeff Davidson in an article in *Bottom Line/Business.* "Don't let papers pile up. File what you need and toss the rest. If information is available elsewhere, don't add it to your files."

An article in the *Record* gives the following filing tips for handling important papers:

⊕ Keep important documents in a safe deposit box. These include mortgage documents, real estate deeds, birth and marriage certificates, citizenship papers, and military service records.

⊕ Create an "active" file. Place in it unpaid bills, receipt of paid bills, bank statements, and canceled checks, income tax working papers, records of charitable donations, and so forth.

⊕ Keep a personal data file including employment records, credit card information, insurance policies, wills, family health records, and social security information.

⊕ Keep a home maintenance notebook that includes appliance manuals and warranties, contractor receipts, and warranties.

☺ Keep an office notebook with copies of computer and office equipment manuals, receipts, warranties, or leases.

Avoid using manila file folders stacked in file-cabinet drawers. These flimsy file folders are difficult to find, and they separate and often slide under one another, making them easy to lose. Use sturdier hanging file folders and file cabinets with high-walled drawers designed to hold these folders. If your file cabinet has regular low-walled drawers, you can buy and easily install adapter brackets to hold the hanging files.

Don't get fancy with file labeling. Use a common-sense labeling scheme and file in alphabetical order. Don't cram files in drawers; this makes them difficult to find and discourages you from even looking. When space gets tight, go through your files, and throw away old and obsolete material—or buy additional file cabinets.

Avoid building stacks of paper on horizontal surfaces. Files should be kept in hanging file folders in a file cabinet or in a series of three-ring binders. If you use binders, label the spines according to the different categories of files (for example, "home," "personal computer," "car," and so forth).

Avoid organizing papers by piling them on your desk. You will quickly clutter your desk and run out of space in which to put fresh stacks. Then you begin putting stacks on top of stacks, which makes it virtually impossible to identify by sight the files in the bottom stacks.

Another flaw of the horizontal-pile filing system is that it can handle an extremely limited amount of files. A typical desk that is 3 feet deep by 7 feet wide, for instance, can only accommodate 30 stacks. If you don't put stacks on stacks, that's a total of only 30 different files.

By comparison, an article in *Law Enforcement Technology* reports that the average four-drawer file cabinet contains 10,000 pieces of paper. If you have 50 sheets per file, that's a total of 200 files. Therefore, your average four-drawer file cabinet can hold almost seven times more files than the top of a table or desk. And the files in the cabinet can't be knocked over by a breeze or clumsy accident.

With file folders removed from your desk, you'll have room for the few active files you need within reach. To organize these files, set up a double or triple-decker in-basket or a separate small set of files for handling incoming paper. I plan my day so I have time every day to go through incoming papers. This way, I can take care of each piece of paper on the spot. If you let papers pile up in in-baskets or to-do files, you may find yourself missing deadlines, payments, and other commitments. Many of the papers will become too old to be meaningful by the time you get to them, and the growing stacks of papers to attend to will become depressing and disheartening.

Paperwork is a necessary evil. To gain greater control over it, decide what to do with each piece of paper as it comes into your office. Then, get rid of it: Pass it along, file it, sign it, revise it, or throw it out. The key is to take action on it right away. Handle each piece of paper as it comes in, and you'll get things done faster, on time, and with less stress.

For the busy business executive or entrepreneur, better organization of paperwork translates directly into getting more done in less time. Poor organization of paper files wastes time and can result in loss of important materials.

Practice the Magic of Saying No

Most of us would rather say yes than no. This may be a result of countless "positive thinking" books and seminars from motivational speakers. Or perhaps it's simply inherent in our nature that we want to please. However, to stay organized and to save time each day, you have to learn to say yes less often and no more often. Although it's scary at first, it's liberating both at work and in your personal life once you put this idea into practice.

Why do you need to say no more often? It's simple: The demand on your time generated by all these requests outweighs the supply. If you say yes to everything others ask of you, you'll have no time for yourself or other things that are very important to you.

Worse, the easiest sin in the world to commit is to over-commit oneself. "Saying no can be a very positive thing," writes David MacAdam, pastor of the New Life Church in Concord, Massachusetts (*www.newlife.org/tgim*). "However, in our culture, it has become a very difficult thing to do." But the penalties for not saying no are even tougher: stress, pressure, overwork, and ultimately missed deadlines and the displeasure of the very people you were seeking to please. MacAdam concludes, "By saying no to the trivial, we can say yes to the important."

The New Bedford Police Department provides local teens with advice for saying no to drinking, smoking, and drugs on their Website: *www. ci.newbedford.ma.us/PSAFETY/POLICE.* With the minor variations added here, these tactics can be equally effective in the business world as well as in most aspects of your personal life:

- ☺ Say "no thanks." When asked, "Would you like to participate in our committee meeting?" simply reply, "No thanks."
- ☺ Give a reason. "Aren't you interested in the committee's work?" your colleague queries. You respond, "Yes, but Tuesday evenings I coach pee-wee soccer" or "I have other commitments."
- ☺ Repeat refusals. Continue to say no politely but firmly. They'll get the message.
- ☺ Walk away. "Can you come to this seminar?" a colleague asks as you are both heading in the direction of the corporate training center. "Sorry, but I can't," you say, and at the corner where the hallways intersect you start walking the other way.
- ☺ Change the subject. "Can we go over these numbers now?" your bookkeeper asks when you have other priorities. You reply, "Can you get me the month-to-date sales figures instead?"
- ☺ Give them the cold shoulder. An effective way to deal with door-to-door and telephone solicitors is simply to say "no, thank you" and close the door or hang up the phone.

Ken Blanchard, co-author of the best-selling book *The One-Minute Manager,* has offered these additional tips for saying no that will keep you on track and save you time in the *Executive Edge Newsletter:*

1. Know what your goals and priorities are. If you have a plan for managing your work and time, it is easier to say no to new activities that don't fit into your agenda. I have a saying in one of my programs: "A person who does not have goals is used by someone who does."

Be clear on your priorities. What are you currently trying to accomplish? By when? How can you focus your energy on things that will move you toward those goals? You have to be somewhat inflexible, as a new assignment or opportunity can be a distraction.

Just let your goals become your reality check. To achieve these goals, you need to set priorities and stick with them. Then you will be better able to discern whether opportunities are important for you at this time in your life.

Good performance always starts with clear goals. Without clear goals you will quickly become a victim of having too many commitments. You will have no framework in which to make decisions about where you should or shouldn't focus your energy.

2. Be realistic about the consequences of doing one more thing. This is both for yourself and for the person who wants your time. The best approach is to be honest and direct. For example, say, "If I do this, I won't be able to get to do the other things that I've committed to" or "With what I've got going on right now, I feel certain that I won't do as good a job as I'd like and we will both be disappointed." When a new opportunity comes your way, compliment the idea (if you feel it has merit) before declining to participate.

3. Offer alternatives and solutions. Suggest someone else who you feel could do a better job or who is available sooner to work on the task. If the request is from your manager, suggest a project or priority that you are doing that could be dropped, delayed, or given to someone else, or ask him or her to suggest an alternative plan.

Which approach you use does, of course, depend on who's asking for your commitment, what the task or project is, and the time frame involved. A request from your manager will involve more consideration and discussion than a request from an associate or someone you don't know.

High performers usually focus on only a few things at a time. Management consultant Peter Drucker asserts that the only people who truly get anything done are monomaniacs—people that intensely focus on one thing at a time. The more you take on, the greater the chance that you will lose effectiveness not only in getting that task done but most likely in all aspects of your life.

Keep in mind that when you say no, you're not saying no to the person, only to the proposition. The people you turn down should not feel insulted. Eleanor Roosevelt said, "Nobody can make you feel inferior without your permission."

There are fates worse than being too busy; one is not being busy enough! For the corporate manager, insufficient workload can spell boredom and be a warning sign that employment is at risk. For the entrepreneur, it can mean slow sales and not enough revenue to meet operating expenses. Being too busy is different from not being busy enough.

Achieve Balance

When you learn to organize your life, you'll find that you have more time—more time not only to get things done at work, but also more time for your personal life. Even with this extra time, achieving a balance between work and home life is for many people a constant struggle.

According to a survey by the Heidrich Center for Work Force Development reported in the *Record* in 1998, 87 percent of workers surveyed said the ability to balance work and family was an "extremely important" job factor. Because work and family compete for the same limited resource—your time—conflict is inevitable.

"We must identify those activities that contribute to our well-being," writes Frank Basile in *Come Fly With Me* (Charisma Publications). "Then we must exclude all other activities...we will have maximum time to spend doing those things which we have consciously identified as being important."

Statistics suggest some factors compensate naturally for the conflict between family and home life. You might, for example, expect married people, especially those with families, to have less time for work than singles. According to an article in *Men's Health* magazine, though, the average married man works 44 hours a week, versus 38 hours a week for the average single man. Perhaps the financial burden of supporting a family compels the married worker to put in more hours to ensure success at the office, or maybe these men stay in the office because it's easier than dealing with problems at home. Whatever the reason, the conflict in balance is apparent.

A key to achieving balance within a limited amount of time is to focus on whatever you are doing at the moment. Don't fret about your weekend date when you're preparing a brief. Don't try to solve work problems in your head while playing a board game with your daughter. "Compartmentalize our different roles," advises Dr. Joyce Brothers in her column in New York's *Daily News* (October 27, 1998). "Then move on to the next task."

When you do tackle problems at work or home, try to find long-term solutions rather than quick fixes and patches. It takes more time up front but can save time in the long run by eliminating repetition of similar problems. "When issues come up, I don't just look to resolve them, I look for solutions so the problems never resurface," says Peter Fioretti, president of Mountain Funding, in *Wealth Building*.

Finally, sometimes to achieve balance, you just have to make tough choices: this instead of that. Information systems professional Jim Geisert, in a letter to the editor in *ComputerWorld*, writes: "It's been a constant struggle to make managers realize my family is more important to me than the next unrealistic deadline. Has my career suffered for it? Absolutely. But it was worth it. I have a happy, healthy daughter who knows she can count on me to be there when she needs me."

Perhaps the headline on the front cover of a Day-Timer catalog—which shows a father hugging his toddler son—says it best: "The most productive meeting time isn't always job related."

Some people complain to me, "Being organized is too much work!" Yes, there's effort involved in setting up systems and changing behaviors to become better organized and more time-efficient. But the long-term reward for being organized returns the short-term investment many times over. Richard J. Leider observes in *The Power of Purpose* (Berrett-Koehler Publishers), "Contrary to many people's thinking, to be organized often means the liberation of time and energy, not the cramping of our style."

Chapter 11

Planning Systems and Software to Increase Your Productivity

Some days you just feel like tearing out what's left of your hair because you can't get it all done! Sound familiar? Then it's time to get life under control with time management tools.

Most of us are so busy every day dealing with our kids, husbands, wives, work and meetings, household chores, and anything else that crops up that it seems like we can't see ahead or figure out what to do next! It's all important! So, now it's just a matter of deciding which chore, or job, comes ahead of another in the schedule.

First, sit down and take stock of your life. Take seven sheets of paper and write on each one, Monday through Sunday, what you know you have to do on a daily basis. Doing it this way at first will show you what occurs on a daily basis and is a routine for you. Then you will see what you do on different days that are recurring weekly, and so forth. After a while, you will see a definite pattern evolving and, if you decide you want to use software to organize everything, then you already have your layouts and know where to enter information once and set a repeat on a daily or weekly basis.

You can start first with wall-based planning calendars if you need to see everything at a glance. These are especially good for project management situations too when you need to follow steps in an orderly manner. Having a visual object to look at to see the overall picture is very important when planning your time. You can get a simple calendar board that allows you to use washable colored ink pens, denoting projects by color across the time span of a project's lifespan. Dry-earse white boards can be drawn on with special ink made for these boards, and then erased with a chalk board eraser, like what we all had in elementary school.

You can also use planner pads that come in many formats and allow you to see events on a weekly to monthly view. For this kind of planning, either software or wall-hanging calendars can work just as well for visual impressions.

Another excellent way to begin getting your life under control and organized is to use a Franklin Planner. Many companies stress training for time and project management for their employees that includes learning and utilizing the Franklin Planner system. In addition to daily pages where you can note your meetings, project progression, and anything else that's part of your life, you can also do goal planning in different sections of the Planner.

There is also a finance planning section, long-term and short-term goals section, contact information, and a section that shows how to use your Franklin Planner. At the end of each month, you will find an expense list where you can log in all expenses made during the month. It allows you to see where you are spending your money and where you might need to cut back.

Additionally, Franklin Covey now offers software packages for your computer and for your cell phone so you can stay in touch constantly with synchronization between applications, including MS Outlook. This allows you to avoid carrying a thick, heavy schedule book around if you would rather not do so. Most people who have used it find they are carrying around their whole life's information—handy, but a little dangerous. Depending on how scatter-brained you might be on any given day, you could possibly leave your planner somewhere and, now, all your important and personal information is gone and someone else has it! You might prefer to just work with the electronic software and synchronizing between applications, which is much safer and allows you to get to your information online, if need be.

Can't afford spending on software right now and need something with a short learning curve? Google Calendar is one of the easiest to use and it is free when you download the Google toolbar. You can set events to repeat day after day or weekly, whatever you choose. In order to get this tool, you do need to sign up for a Gmail (e-mail) account. Your calendar will send you reminders to your Gmail in-box when an event is coming up. The settings system can be set to notify you an hour ahead so you have time to get ready, just in case you forgot!

If you already have Microsoft Office with MS Outlook, then use the calendar section in Outlook. If you start out with either one of those, know that you can now interchange or update your online Google calendar from Outlook, or reverse the settings to update your Outlook calendar from Google. You can also set your options to update in both directions simultaneously. Or, you can even arrange it where Google Calendar will show you only your business appointments, which will then download to your Outlook Calendar, where it combines with your personal appointments that you need to get done.

I suggest Google Calendar to start because it is free and easy to use, especially if you've never used online calendars before and you don't have Outlook right now. Using Google calendar will help you with managing your time for now until you need something more advanced. You also have access to a notes section in the calendar where you can make lists of the projects you have coming up, items that you need to purchase, or any other notes you need to make, which can be seen every single day. You can then check off each item when completed.

If you don't want to use Google Calendar, then look up a list of time-management software on the Internet. Some are free and simple to use, although they may or may not have the same interactive downloading abilities as Google with MS Outlook. As I write, software is changing rapidly and what may not be available today, could possibly hit the market tomorrow!

If you would like to try Microsoft Outlook 2007, you can download a free two-month trial of MS Office 2007 on your computer and pay some $450–500 at the end of the trial in order to keep access to all your work. It does give you time to play with the software and see what it does for you. Included in the Business 2007 trial version are Outlook with Contact Manager, Word, Excel, PowerPoint and Publisher, with some MS business tools thrown in as well. The Outlook program is more advanced than Google but, rather than fearing to work with this program, use online help to get you started. The investment in learning how to use this program will be worth your time in the long run. You can purchase your trial version and then upgrade to get Access, too, which is a heavy-duty database, best used by expert "tweakers" and programmers who know how to do macros and design database formulae behind the scenes.

One of the big features of Outlook 2007 with Contact Manager is that you can develop your own marketing database list within the manager by including all information for each contact with phone, fax, address, city, state, zip code, e-mail address, and anything else you need to include. You can also pull reports by information you have included, which can be sorted by the criteria you requested in the query. It is almost a mini version of Access in its database capabilities, and all your information can be transferred over to Access if you wish to use that also. For now, stick with Outlook until you are an expert user of that program first.

Another popular customer contact database program is ACT!, now owned by Sage. The latest version is ACT! 2010, and this program will also interact with Outlook 2007/2010. The best way to learn how to do the transfer of information and integration of e-mail send outs is to try out the ACT! trial version along with your MS Outlook trial version. Use the help files and training videos provided with the software, and also look at the software's home Website for more helpful information. By the time both trial versions are up, you will have a pretty good idea of whether you can save a lot of time (and money) by using the interactivity of both software packages. Big note to self: Back up all your files but also export information in databases and spreadsheets into comma delimited files so that, if you choose not to continue with those software programs, you can import the information into another program, like Open Office, which is free.

Suppose you're just starting out in business and barely have a penny left to spend on software business tools. Open Office, by SUN Microsystems, is the best freebie on the market. You can download the whole series of programs in one go, and then open any program you want from the common starting menu that asks you which program you want to use. One of the best features of Open Office is that you can save your files into a compatible file that MS Office users can open and convert to their programs. You will definitely need to check to see what version of MS Office your client has before sending your files by e-mail. If your client needs to make revisions and send the file back to you, then it will need to be saved in the same original format so you can open it back up to do any editing.

Again, take the time to learn this program through the help files, online tutorials, and anything else that SUN offers on its Website in terms of training and latest operating tips. As with MS Office and most other software programs, you can also go to your local bookstore and find books that will show you how to use your software. Tight on available cash? Make a list of the books you find that will be helpful to you, and then go to Amazon. com to pull up those same books. In most cases, they will be cheaper online and, over a certain ordering amount, will qualify for free ground UPS shipping. You can also ask for overnight or two-day shipping for an extra fee, of course, if you are in a rush.

Personally, I like to look through books and see what's in them before purchasing. Also, I am a fan of local bookstores and like to support their continued existence, so occasionally I purchase a book there, too. Remember that most of these places have coffee shops where you can set up your laptop to do your research and work on their Internet access server—for free. Additionally, you can pull books from the shelves and take them to your table, where you are set up with your laptop, so you can do more refined research—for free. This arrangement also saves you time and money, and can help you in getting more done faster. One just hopes a gaggle of school kids won't come in to sit down and ruin your peace and quiet! Of course, on the other side of that, it's great they congregate in a bookstore where they might just pick up a book, and do some reading, and learn something new!

Back to time management. If you are going the cheap way, you now have Google Calendar, access to Google Documents, and a host of free tools to use for your online office needs. You have Open Office as your main working office suite of business programs, and you've learned how to use both software programs and features. If you are able to spend a bit of money, you've downloaded MS Office 2007 free (for now), as well as the Google Toolbar with Calendar and Documents, and so forth. What next in your toolkit line-up?

Do you need to purchase a phone for business communication? Then buy one of the latest on the market that acts just like a mini-computer on steroids. Motorola Droid and Cliq, Apple iPhone and iPad, and Blackberry Curve and Bold are just a few types out on the market that have abilities to synchronize with your online Google and Outlook calendar programs. These phones are capable of an amazing array of functions that help you save time *and* money by taking care of business quickly and easily.

As a mini-computer of sorts, you can pay bills through your online service, find where the nearest Wal-mart is located and get directions from where you are currently (by GPS), pick up text messages and e-mails, socialize with your Twitter and Facebook friends, and a host of other operations. If you are in an area where you can't get Internet access through your laptop, then hook up your phone and you are under way again, riding on your phone power and Internet access to find what you need. Mind you, while doing this you should keep your phone charged as you are using a lot of battery power. Also, although GPS capabilities are great most of the time, be aware that *someone* knows where you are at any given time, just by accessing your GPS locator remotely.

On another note, whatever phone you end up purchasing, definitely check out any available "apps" that have been created to work with your phone. There are so many out there right now, and they are all designed to make your life easier and to accomplish things faster, such as paying bills on the run. You can check bank balances, get news updates, get weather updates (really great in hurricane season!), get traffic updates on your regular travel route, and it goes on. Every day there is a new app created, but I recommend you check out reviews and other information about what your app can do before you download it to your phone or in some cases, your computer desktop. Some are free to download and others require only a small amount to purchase.

Social media has come a long way to the forefront of worldwide communications. You can easily market your products and services by just making yourself visible to your contacts in the groups like Twitter and Facebook, to name a few. With constant updates that show up on your followers' sites, you are constantly reminding everyone of what you are doing and what you can offer to your potential clients. All of this can be done through your phone, but a word of caution here: If you are a busy working person, you may not want to activate the social media links, as you will get constant updates from your followers, too. Constant distraction while working is not what you need! Your option settings can be set where the social media applications are turned off. Then once or twice a day, manually log in to see what's going on and send out notices of your own.

Project management tools have also improved over time, with more developed features and benefits, allowing you to keep track of project hours and subsequent billing procedures. If you have a business that requires you charge by the hour, then use a software program that can help you do that easily for you.

Here is a comparison of notable project management software from Wikipedia, the free online encyclopedia. Though many of these may work better for large business companies, there will be a few suitable for a new small business to use. Take a look at several comparisons to see which one can help you the most with your particular business needs. See if you can download free trials so you can work with them and see which one is to your liking.

Software	Collaborative software	Issue tracking system	Scheduling	Project portfolio management	Resource management	Document management	Web-based	License
24SevenOffice	Yes	No	No	No	No	No	Yes	Proprietary
Assembla	Yes	Yes	No	Yes	Yes	Yes	Yes	Proprietary
AtTask	Yes	Yes	Yes	Yes	Yes	Yes	Yes	Proprietary
Basecamp	Yes	No	No	No	Yes	Yes	Yes	Proprietary
Central Desktop	Yes	Yes	No	No	No	Yes	Yes	Proprietary
Cerebro	Yes	Yes	Yes	No	Yes	Yes	Yes	Proprietary
Clarizen	Yes	Yes	Yes	Yes	Yes	Yes	Yes	Proprietary
codeBeamer	Yes	Yes	No	No	No	Yes	Yes	Proprietary
Collabtive	Yes	No	No	No	No	No	Yes	Open source
Contactizer	Yes	No	No	No	Yes	No	No	Proprietary
Daptiv	Yes	Yes	Yes	Yes	Yes	Yes	Yes	Proprietary
dotProject	No	Yes	No	No	No	Yes	Yes	Open source

Software	Collaborative software	Issue tracking system	Scheduling	Project portfolio management	Resource management	Document management	Web-based	License
Endeavour Software Project Management	Yes	Yes	Yes	Yes	Yes	Yes	Yes	Open source
Easy Projects .NET	Yes	Yes	Yes	Yes	Yes	Yes	Yes	Proprietary
eGroupWare	Yes	Yes	No	Yes	Yes	Yes	Yes	Proprietary
FastTrack Schedule	No	No	Yes	No	Yes	No	No	Proprietary
Feng Office Community Edition	Yes	No	Yes	Yes	No	Yes	Yes	Open source
FogBugz	Yes	Yes	Yes	No	Yes	No	Yes	Proprietary
GanttProject	No	No	Yes	No	Yes	No	No	Open source
Gemini	Yes	Yes	Yes	No	Yes	Yes	Yes	Proprietary
Genius Inside	Yes	Yes	Yes	Yes	Yes	Yes	Yes	Proprietary
Glasscubes	Yes	Yes	No	No	No	Yes	Yes	Proprietary
Huddle	Yes	No	No	No	No	Yes	Yes	Proprietary
Hyperoffice	Yes	No	No	No	No	Yes	Yes	Proprietary
InLoox	Yes	Yes	Yes	No	Yes	Yes	No	Proprietary
JIRA	Yes	Yes	No	No	No	No	Yes	Proprietary
Journyx	Yes	Yes	Yes	Yes	Yes	Yes	Yes	Proprietary
Kayako helpdesk software	Yes	Yes	No	No	No	Yes	Yes	Proprietary
KForge	Yes	Yes	No	No	No	Yes	Yes	Open source
KKOOP	Yes	No	No	No	No	Yes	Yes	Proprietary
KPlato	No	No	No	No	Yes	No	No	Open source
Launchpad	Yes	Yes	No	Yes	No	No	Yes	Open source
LiquidPlanner	Yes	No	Yes	Yes	Yes	Yes	Yes	Proprietary
LisaProject	No	No	Yes	No	Yes	No	No	Proprietary
MacProject	No	No	Yes	No	Yes	No	No	Proprietary
MantisBT	Yes	Yes	Yes	No	No	Yes	Yes	Open source
MatchWare MindView 3 Business	Yes	No	Yes	Yes	Yes	Yes	Yes	Proprietary
Merlin	Yes	Yes	Yes	Yes	Yes	Yes	Yes	Proprietary
MicroPlanner X-Pert	Yes	Yes	Yes	Yes	Yes	No	No	Proprietary
Microsoft Office Project Server	Yes	Yes	Yes	Yes	Yes	Yes	Yes	Proprietary
Microsoft Project	No	No	Yes	No	Yes	No	No	Proprietary
Mingle	Yes	Yes	No	No	No	No	Yes	Proprietary
O3spaces	Yes	No	No	No	No	Yes	No	Proprietary
OmniPlan	No	No	Yes	No	Yes	No	No	Proprietary

Software	Collaborative software	Issue tracking system	Scheduling	Project portfolio management	Resource management	Document management	Web-based	License
Open Workbench	No	No	Yes	No	Yes	No	No	Open source
OpenProj	No	No	Yes	No	Yes	No	No	Open source
Oracle Project Portfolio Management	Yes	Yes	Yes	Yes	Yes	Yes	Yes	Proprietary
Planisware 5	Yes	Yes	Yes	Yes	Yes	Yes	Yes	Proprietary
Planner Suite	No	No	Yes	Yes	Yes	Yes	No	Proprietary
Primavera Project Planner	Yes	Yes	Yes	Yes	Yes	Yes	Yes	Proprietary
Project KickStart	No	No	Yes	No	Yes	No	No	Proprietary
Project.net	Yes	Yes	Yes	Yes	Yes	Yes	Yes	Open source
Project-Open	Yes	Yes	Yes	Yes	Yes	Yes	Yes	Open source
Projectplace	Yes	Yes	Yes	Yes	No	Yes	Yes	Proprietary
ProjectSpaces	Yes	Yes	Yes	No	No	Yes	Yes	Proprietary
Projektron BCS	Yes	Yes	Yes	Yes	Yes	Yes	Yes	Proprietary
PSNext	Yes	Yes	Yes	Yes	Yes	Yes	Yes	Proprietary
QuickBase	Yes	Yes	No	Yes	Yes	Yes	Yes	Proprietary
Redmine	Yes	Yes	Yes	Yes	No	Yes	Yes	Open source
Rachota	No	Yes	No	No	No	No	No	Open source
SAP RPM	Yes	Yes	Yes	Yes	Yes	Yes	Yes	Proprietary
Severa	Yes	Yes	Yes	Yes	Yes	Yes	Yes	Proprietary
SharpForge (Defunct)	Yes	Yes	No	No	No	Yes	Yes	Open source
Smartsheet	Yes	Yes	No	Yes	Yes	Yes	Yes	Proprietary
TaskJuggler	Yes	No	Yes	No	Yes	No	No	Open source
Teamcenter	Yes	Yes	Yes	Yes	Yes	No	No	Proprietary
Teamwork	Yes	Yes	Yes	Yes	Yes	Yes	Yes	Proprietary
Teamwork PM	Yes	Yes	Yes	Yes	Yes	Yes	Yes	Proprietary
Tenrox	Yes	Yes	Yes	Yes	Yes	Yes	Yes	Proprietary
Trac	Yes	Yes	No	No	No	No	Yes	Open source
TrackerSuite.Net	Yes	Yes	Yes	Yes	Yes	Yes	Yes	Proprietary
Ubidesk	Yes	Yes	Yes	No	No	Yes	Yes	Proprietary
VPMi	Yes	Yes	Yes	Yes	Yes	No	Yes	Proprietary
WorkLenz	Yes	Yes	Yes	Yes	Yes	Yes	Yes	Proprietary
WorkPLAN Enterprise	Yes	No	Yes	Yes	Yes	Yes	No	Proprietary
workspace.com	Yes	Yes	Yes	Yes	Yes	Yes	Yes	Proprietary
WebSPOC	Yes	Yes	No	Yes	Yes	No	Yes	Proprietary
Wrike	Yes	Yes	Yes	No	No	No	Yes	Proprietary
Zoho Projects	Yes	No	No	No	Yes	Yes	Yes	Proprietary

Source: *en.wikipedia.org/wiki/Comparison_of_project_management_software*

If you don't want to tackle something too complicated right off the bat, then Google has a number of apps (short for applications) that can integrate with some of your other Google tools. First, do a Google search with the phrase "project management software free," and then click on the link for Google Apps Project Management (marketplace). A listing of 10 applications will pull up, and you can sort through the descriptions to see which ones will work for you. Most will allow you to download a trial version, giving you enough time to learn how it works and see if it works for you.

One free Google application, with no download of software, is Manymoon. If you already have your Google account, then when you get to Manymoon's home page at *www.manymoon.com,* you will just sign in under Google Accounts. You may need to verify your e-mail address through Google mail first, but once that is done, you will go right to your projects page. Here you can select on the left side whether you want to add a new project, send a bulletin, enter in tasks, upload documents to Google Doc, and allow access to other users. You can also add your hours working for a project, making it very helpful at invoice time. It is an amazing application and certainly great for first-time users in need of a synchronized time-management tool.

If you need a larger resource, then you have the option to upgrade to Manymoon Team, which has two different plans with a monthly charge from $10 to $20, but allows more options for you to use. If your business calendar requires you to interact with many clients over a number of different projects, then upgrading to the monthly charge program of choice would be time- and cost-effective for you. You can start out with the free version and then move up without loss of information on previous projects.

Another free software program is Open Workbench, which claims to be a "MS Project software killer," according to its online description. You can download your free software from the home site and also download a user guide in Adobe Acrobat's Reader software. (The Acrobat reader is also free if you don't already have it. Go to *www.adobe.com* to download the latest version.) Once you have downloaded Open Workbench, create your profile at the home page so you can have access to training information and to review FAQs. For instance, you can save an Open Workbench file as an .xml and then have your client's MS Project Manager import the file into its program. Just remember that the file must be saved with the same extension in order for your Open Workbench to open it back up. This is only in cases where a client might be using Project and you are using Open Workbench, or in reverse.

Another software package to mention is SmartDraw, which you can download as a free trial with option to purchase later. This is another great visual tool that has many applications, with time and project management being just one of its many features. You can also download a manual to help with training so you are not just spinning wheels once you've got it on your computer. The price to buy is also very reasonable, considering what it is capable of doing for you.

Now you have a whole array of planning options to choose from. Take the time to try different options but get yourself going on some kind of time and project management system. You'll be grateful if you find yourself really busy and not worrying how to keep track of it all and satisfy your clients too. That's because you are now a time management professional. Your clients will love you for it!

Research Links

Free Stuff

freelanceswitch.com/productivity/8-simple-online-time-management-tools-for-freelancers

www.vitalist.com

todoist.com

download.openoffice.org (Free office suite of business tools when you can't afford MS Office. An amazing program for FREE! Has a text program, spreadsheet, presentation, database, drawing programs included, and is easy to use when learning through help files.)

www.openworkbench.org (Free project management software.)

www.adobe.com (Download your free pdf reader here.)

Project and Network Management

www.backpackit.com

www.google.com (When you set up an account here, you have calendar, documents stored online, notes, and a host of other free available tools to use for managing your time. Start with this and then when you need something more advanced, check out software packages.)

www.basecamphq.com

www.daytimer.com (Home site for Daytimer information and ordering.)

www.shelltoys.com/download.html (Downloads of Daytimer and accessories)

www.franklincovey.com (Information on planners and time management software offerings.)

Customer Relationship Management (CRM)

www.bigcontacts.com (Do everything online and access it anywhere in the world. Free trial only.)

www.highrisehq.com (More CRM online. Free trial only.)

Miscellaneous

www.timetimer.com/applications/business.php (Purchase your unique timer here to time meetings, phone calls, and other time managed events.)

www.home-organization-online.com (Some good planning tips for home and home offices.)

www.squidoo.com/time-management-planner (Tips on planning and time management.)

www.magnatag.com/page/PROJECT/category.asp (Go here to look at different systems of wall-based planning and project-management calendars that you can order. Ranging from colored pens to magnetic features that allow you to see at a glance where a project is and where it needs to go next.)

www.smartdraw.com/downloads (Go here to get your SmartDraw download!)

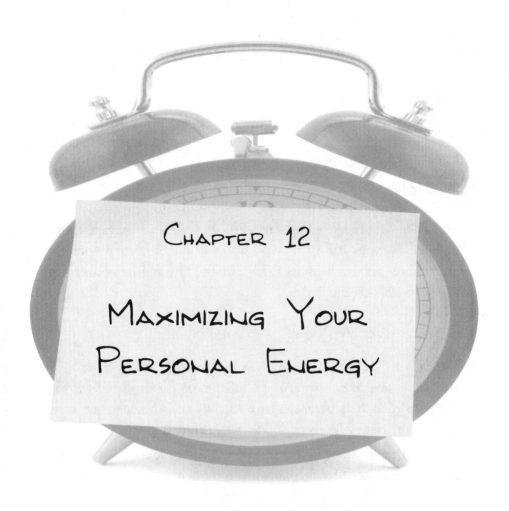

CHAPTER 12

MAXIMIZING YOUR
PERSONAL ENERGY

"Time is as elusive as a thief, silent as death."
—Mumia Abu-Jamal

The pace today is brutal. You need maximum energy just to keep up. Yet most of us don't have enough energy available to fuel the super-productivity we may wish to achieve in the time available to do it.

This energy drain often stems from the growing societal demand to literally make every second count. According to a study from the Future Foundation (a London-based think tank), we are rapidly approaching a 24-hour society. "The World Wide Web, fax machines, and other information technology make it possible to operate around the clock, increasing the pressure to do so," says an article in the *Futurist*. The result is increased customer demand to have services available at all hours.

Coping with this frantic pace can be draining at times. This chapter explores some ideas to help boost your energy level so you can think better and concentrate longer, and thus make the most of the time you choose to dedicate to both work and play.

"The average person puts only 25 percent of his energy and ability to work," Andrew Carnegie complained in a *Bits & Pieces* magazine article. "The world takes its hat off to those who put in more than 50 percent of their capacity and stands on its head for those few-and-far-between souls who devote 100 percent."

Re-Energize Yourself

I admit it: I'm tired. Fortunately, I have enough energy to do the one thing I really love to do: work. But I collapse on evenings and weekends. That's not a good thing because I have a family and a home to take care of. Increasing my energy level is a short-term goal for me.

I know I'm not alone in this situation. Many people I talk to complain that today's fast pace tires them out and robs them of energy. "If energy is the currency of life, many of us have little left in reserve," writes Melissa Diane Smith in her article "Energy to Spare" in *Delicious!* "We've dipped into our storage bank so often and pushed ourselves so much that we're simply energy depleted."

Here are some ideas for increasing your energy levels:

- ⊕ Get a check-up. As Laurie M. Aesoph observes in her article "Nutrients that Energize" in *Health & Nutrition Breakthroughs,* "Fatigue is a symptom, not a disease." Therefore, if you suffer from constant fatigue, a trip to your family physician may be a good idea.

- ⊕ Factors that can contribute to low energy include: lack of sleep, stress, poor eating habits, too little water, lack of exercise, and side effects from prescription drugs. Arthritis, heart disease, hypothyroidism, obesity, depression, cancer, and other diseases can also diminish energy.

Do you suffer from chronic fatigue? The causes of chronic fatigue syndrome (CFS) are not well understood. Neither are the treatments. However, as the name implies, those who suffer from CFS are chronically exhausted and need specialized medical attention.

If you are always tired, your physician might also check for mitochondrial dysfunction. Mitochondria supply the body with energy by metabolically breaking down protein, carbohydrate, and fat in cells. A number of factors, including stress, changes in diet, environmental toxins, or over-exertion, can interfere with this energy production.

If you're wasting time every day because you're just too tired to concentrate or focus, see your doctor. There may very well be a medical reason for your fatigue.

☻ Eat light and right. Big meals can make you sleepy. What is the reason? Depending on your diet, 50 to 80 percent of the energy produced by digesting food is consumed by the act of digestion itself. The more energy that digestion takes, the less energy the food provides the rest of your body. It takes more energy to digest cooked and processed food and much less to digest fruits, vegetables, grains, and nuts. Try to eat more of the latter. They're easier on your digestive system and you gain more energy from them.

If your diet doesn't give you this amount of fresh food, you can juice the fruits and vegetables. Or you can take concentrated fruits and vegetables in capsule form. (Water is taken out of living fruits and vegetables through a drying process involving vacuum, pressure, and temperature. The remaining dry powder is put in capsules with no chemical additives.)

Diet also affects our adrenal glands, which produce hormones that help balance blood sugar. Blood sugar level determines whether we have the right amount of fuel to meet our varying demands for energy. In situations that demand high energy, such as flight from danger, the adrenals release hormones to generate this additional energy. Fatigue is a major symptom of adrenal dysfunction. Other symptoms include poor sleep, low stamina, an inability to concentrate, low immune function, poor digestion, and an inability to cope with stress.

You can boost the health of your adrenal glands through diet. Eat a well-balanced diet, with protein, fat, and carbohydrates at each meal. This will promote the healthy production of blood sugar, which helps maintain energy levels.

If you know your diet isn't giving you the nutrients you need to stay sharp, talk to your doctor about taking vitamin and mineral supplements. These can help fill in the gaps and keep you going.

🕐 Reduce caffeine and sugar. Caffeine and sugar aren't particularly healthy. However, I admit to using both as short-term energy boosters—in moderation, of course.

Sugar has virtually no nutritional value. Eating sugar tends to rob the body of its nutrient stores. It also causes drastic swings in blood sugar levels, stressing the adrenal glands. Coffee, which can give you a temporary lift in energy, also weakens the adrenals.

Given these facts, here's how I use sugar and caffeine: I know I'm going to consume a certain amount of both. Because they do give a natural energy lift, I eat or drink them at those times I know I want the energy boost they provide, and I avoid them at other times of day.

For instance, like many people, I drink coffee in the morning for the caffeine stimulation. But unlike many people, I don't drink another cup after dinner. After all, why would I want another caffeine shot when I'm relaxing in the evening and getting ready to go to bed?

The approximate caffeine content of popular caffeine-containing foods and drinks are listed here:

Item	Average mg of caffeine
Coffee (5 oz. cup)	
Brewed by drip method	115 mg
Brewed by percolator	80 mg
Instant	65 mg
Tea (5 oz. cup)	
Brewed	40 mg
Instant	30 mg
Iced (12-oz. cup)	70 mg

Item	Average mg of caffeine
Chocolate bar (6 oz.)	25 mg
Chocolate milk (1 oz.)	6 mg
Coca-Cola	46 mg
Excedrin	65 mg
Dristan tablets	16 mg

Source: Reprinted by permission from *Insomnia: 50 Essential Things to Do* (Penguin Group) by Theresa Foy DiGeronimo.

As for sugar, I sometimes have a small candy bar or cookie in the mid-afternoon, the period when my energy most often wanes. I don't eat candy as a snack at any other time, and I rarely have cookies or cake for dessert. This limited indulgence keeps me happy and at the same time helps me avoid the energy-zapping effects of too much sugar.

Practice Feng Shui: Energy in the Workplace

Can you literally increase your energy by rearranging the furniture in your office? Believe it or not, practitioners of feng shui think so.

Feng shui (pronounced FUNG SHWAY), a 3,000-year-old Chinese discipline for harmonious interior design, has had a stateside revival in recent years and is transforming the surroundings of business executives across the country. What some may regard as New Age touchy-feely nonsense has been embraced wholeheartedly by the likes of Donald Trump, Tommy Hilfiger, Madonna, and Steve Martin. In the workplace, the teachings of feng shui are improving employee relations and increasing overall productivity.

"When people call me, they want to increase their profits and their prosperity," says Carole Bollini, a consultant who runs Enlightened Environment in Oakland, New Jersey, in an article in *Business News.* By adding foliage or water fountains, by repositioning furniture, or by reconstructing entire rooms, feng shui consultants and their clients try to lift and guide spirits to produce results.

The term *feng shui* translates into English as wind and water. The teachings center around the notion that the design of a room can represent a particular theme, such as relationships, careers, or prosperity. It is used to affect personal emotions and energy, which, according to feng shui philosophy, flow like the wind and water, in a positive way.

The art began to appear in the United States in California, where it was introduced by migrating Chinese masters. "It's just beginning to come into more focus on the East Coast," says Bollini, who has been a practicing consultant since 1996. Here are some of the principles of this art:

- **Water.** "Water fountains are placed in the front entrance of a business or to the left to enhance the career section of the room," says Valerie Bogdan, a consultant who runs Feng Shui Works out of her Somerset, New Jersey, home in the *Business News* article. Each year, Bogdan advises 15 corporate clients, including AT&T and Merrill Lynch, 100 small business owners, and 200 homeowners. "Water is a sign of prosperity and generates a relaxed calm connection to nature," she adds.

- **Space.** One practice of feng shui is known as space clearing—basically the philosophy of out with the old and in with the new. Articles of furniture and miscellaneous items that are cluttering space are removed, and the consultant clears the area of negative energies by walking around the room to spread the fumes from smoldering sage sticks. The pleasing scent and the removal of old junk infuse positive energy into the room. "Clutter," says Bollini, "causes stagnation."

  Space constraints can also have a negative impact on employee motivation, according to Bollini: "Being surrounded by computers, squashing too many people into your back to the door makes you subconsciously think about being surprised and that is a drain on energy."

- **Art.** Bogdan sometimes needs to help her clients liven up their walls. "Some of the artwork at corporations is cold and hostile. They will have abstract or very confusing pictures. I find that to be the most negative," says Bogdan. To ease employee spirits she recommends images of lighthearted and nature-oriented scenes, such as children playing or sunsets.

⊕ **Light.** Lighting also plays a factor on the state of mind, according to both Bollini and Bogdan. They find that the oppressive feel of fluorescent lighting can be countered with full spectrum light. That gives the effect of true daylight indoors, thus bringing a sense of nature back into the workplace.

Monitor Your Sleep

Numerous studies indicate that most people need eight hours of sleep, yet an increasing number get far less. We are working longer, staying up later, and getting up earlier. For instance, the Future Foundation study found a 20-percent increase in British television viewing between 3 a.m. and 6 a.m., according to *The Futurist.* The result is an increasing number of people who can't focus. Anyone who has ever pulled an "all-nighter" to cram for an exam or a presentation knows that sleep deprivation dulls your mental edge.

Workers who sleep less so they can work more and get more done may in fact be accomplishing the opposite. The National Sleep Foundation estimates overtired employees cost American business $18 billion annually in errors and slowness, according to an article in *Forbes.*

A major cause of poor sleep among busy professionals is ruminating, which is the practice of thinking about work problems when you're not at work. Many professionals I have talked with tell me that Sunday night is miserable for them because all they do is think about the problems they have to deal with on Monday morning. They toss and turn, and get little sleep. Some even say work nightmares dominate their dreams!

What's the solution? Clear your mind of all your worries before you go to bed each night. Writing in *Professional Speaker,* Angela Brown suggests you make a list of things on your mind, leave that list on your nightstand, and don't allow yourself to think about any of them until morning. "Once you release your have-tos and should-haves from your conscious mind, you'll enjoy a deeper sleep," says Brown. "When you awaken, you'll be refreshed and ready to tackle the list with renewed enthusiasm."

My sister, Fern, has a different solution for coping with her Sunday-night worries: She often goes into the office for a few hours Sunday night.

"I'm going to worry anyway, so while this stuff is on my mind, I'd rather be at my desk getting it organized and done," says Fern. An added benefit of Fern's Sunday night work session is a reduced workload for Monday mornings, which in turn helps lower her stress levels.

Here are some additional tips for getting a good night's sleep:

☺ Drink no more than five cups of caffeinated drinks a day and none in the four hours before bedtime.

☺ Cut down on smoking. Nicotine is a central nervous system stimulant that can make it difficult to fall asleep, and, because it's addictive, cravings may wake you in the middle of the night.

☺ Avoid a nightcap. Alcohol has an initial sedative effect. However, it causes arousals and sleep fragmentation during the night that lower the quality and restorative power of sleep.

☺ Beware of the sleep-disturbing effects of many over-the-counter and prescription drugs. Medications that can disrupt sleep include those that contain caffeine, such as Excedrin, Anacin, or Triaminic, many antidepressant drugs, some birth-control pills, some broncho-dilating drugs for asthma, steroid preparations, some drugs for high blood pressure, and many diet pills.

☺ Try to keep a consistent daily schedule. Rise and sleep at the same time every day.

☺ Stay away from sleeping pills. These pills cause tolerance, which requires you to use more and more for the same effect. They can increase sleeplessness when they are discontinued, and they can be addictive and cause withdrawal symptoms when they are discontinued.

Try Relaxation Techniques

Relaxation techniques are activities that help you relax when you want to so that you can recharge your batteries and have energy when you need to.

There are many ways to relax. Stephen King, best-selling horror novelist, reads fiction to unwind. "People sometimes overlook the restorative power of stories," said King in a speech at a booksellers' convention I attended.

Fiction is escape—and relaxation. Most popular forms of entertainment—books, videos, movies, TV shows—are based around stories. So the right relaxation technique for you might be as simple as curling up with a good mystery. Even many rock songs tell a story, and most video games have a plot.

Some people practice yoga—known for its ability to reduce stress and increase mental discipline and concentration—to relax. "The word 'yoga' conjures up many images, including emaciated Indians in contorted postures, swallowing rags, levitating above the ground, and meditating for unreasonably long periods of time," says yoga teacher Kathleen Miller. "In reality, yoga is a physical discipline involving particular postures and possibly some breathing techniques."

In the United States the most common yoga practice is hatha yoga, which involves mainly the body and breath. According to Miller, hatha yoga's effects of relaxation, increased flexibility, strength, vitality, improved concentration, and immune system function have been well-documented.

Another very popular relaxation technique is transcendental meditation (TM). According to books and literature from the Maharishi Vedic University (*www.maharishi.org*), the TM technique is a simple, natural, effortless procedure practiced for 15–20 minutes in the morning and evening, while sitting comfortably with the eyes closed.

During TM, the individual experiences a unique state of restful alertness. As the body becomes relaxed, the mind transcends all mental activity to experience the simplest form of awareness, called "Transcendental Consciousness." Practitioners claim that this practice dissolves accumulated stress and fatigue through the deep rest gained during the practice. This, in turn, helps practitioners achieve greater effectiveness and success in daily life.

The Vedic University reports that more than 500 scientific research studies conducted during the past 25 years at more than 200 independent universities and research institutes in 30 countries have shown that the TM program benefits all areas of an individual's life: mind, body, behavior, and environment. The research has been published in numerous scientific journals including *Science, Scientific American,* and the *International Journal of Neuroscience.*

🕐 🕐 🕐 🕐

10 Ways to Reduce Stress

Life can be a pressure cooker. Too much stress not only harms personal productivity; it can be costly too. A survey by the Health Enhancement Research Organization reported in *American Demographics* reveals that people who said they were under constant stress had medical expenditures 46 percent higher than people without such stress, which cost businesses an extra $2,287 per year each per employee.

In addition to the relaxation techniques mentioned earlier, here are 10 simple techniques you can use to reduce stress and tension.

1. **Hobbies.** The best way to take your mind off your work is with a hobby that fills your free time. Pick a hobby that offers you something you can't get on the job. For example, if you sit at a desk all day, try hiking, camping, bicycle riding, or some other physical activity. If you feel your job doesn't provide an outlet for your creativity, take up painting, music, or another activity that satisfies your creative side.

2. **Vacations.** Many people boast of going years without a vacation. This is a sign of trouble—not commitment. Sitting on the beach, under the sun, with the waves pounding at your feet is a marvelous way to let off some of the pressure that builds up in the work environment.

   According to *Sales & Marketing Management* (March 1999), a 1999 study from Hyatt Hotels & Resorts revealed that 63 percent of executives said periodic, one-week vacations were essential to maintaining a positive attitude at work. In fact, 73 percent of executives surveyed said they'd rather pass up a 10-percent pay raise than give up a week of vacation time.

   How long should your vacation be? It depends on your personality. Some people find they need at least a week or two to unwind fully. Others say taking that much time off creates a backlog of work that just adds to their stress when they return to the job. Those people may be better off with several short vacations throughout the year.

3. **Screening.** If you find constant interruptions stressful, it may pay to screen calls and visitors. Take calls when you want to; if you're busy, have someone take a message so you can return the call later.

4. **An unlisted phone number.** Few things are as intrusive as a work-related phone call received at home. If you are bothered by too many such calls from subordinates or supervisors, consider getting an unlisted number. If company policy dictates that people at work must have access to your home number, you might want to buy a telephone answering machine or let voice mail pick up your incoming calls (then retrieve the message and decide whether to respond). Another option is to get Caller ID. When the phone rings, the LED shows who the call is from. Then you decide whether to take it or let the voice mail answer.

5. **Privacy.** Modular offices and open work spaces are popular with managers who think constant employee interaction is a good thing. These set-ups deprive workers of privacy, and lack of privacy in turn adds stress and reduces productivity. Consider an office set-up in which all of your employees have small, private offices, with doors they can easily shut. Small inner offices give each employee a quiet place to think.

6. **Dual offices.** My Uncle Max, a college professor, has two offices: his regular office and a small, "secret" office tucked away in the basement of another department's building. Max goes to the hidden office to unwind and to work away from the crowds for a few hours when the pressures of students, faculty meetings, and research begin to overwhelm him.

7. **Delegation.** Do you have too much work to do? Delegate it. Don't think you're the only one who can do your work. You'd be surprised at what your co-workers can accomplish for you.

8. **Dividing and conquering.** If you're faced with a big task and a short deadline, break up the assignment into many smaller segments and do a part of the job every day. Having to write only one page a day for 10 days seems a lot less formidable a task than having to produce a 10-page paper in two weeks.

9. **Deep breathing.** Psychologists have developed a number of relaxation techniques that can help reduce stress on the job. All of these techniques can be performed easily at work. One of the most basic techniques is deep breathing. It relieves stress and tension by increasing your oxygen intake. To practice it, sit in a comfortable position with your hands on your stomach. Inhale deeply and slowly.

Let your stomach expand as much as possible. Hold your breath for five seconds. Then, exhale slowly through pursed lips, as if you were whistling. Repeat the cycle three or four times.

10. **Visualizations.** To escape from the stress of the "real world," close your door, sit back, and spend the next 10 minutes in a pleasant daydream. This short "mental vacation" provides a nice tension-reducing break.

⏲   ⏲   ⏲   ⏲

Use Productive Energy in Intense, Short Bursts

In Chapter 1, we talked about the strategy of breaking your day into one-hour work segments. In addition to organizing your activity for the day, the "hour power" method has another benefit: It gives you added energy to get more done.

One or two hours turns out to be the perfect work increment: It seems to be the optimum period of time for working with intense concentration. Why? Research shows that you suffer a loss of stamina after 90 to 120 minutes of focused activity. After that time, the body needs a break to induce the biological changes that restore energy.

With this method, not only do you maximize your energy, but you focus it on one task. The result is that you make significant headway on that task in only one to two hours. The breaks between your intense work sessions need not be long; two to five minutes can re-energize you for the next one or two hours.

With this method of maximizing energy, you make every second count for a specific block of time, then recharge and get back to productive work. This is a great time-management technique that uses both intense and relaxed time to complement each other.

After the last hour of intense work, mentally reward yourself with a break—for the entire evening. Don't carry around the burdens of work after you have left your office for the night. Write them on tomorrow's to-do list, post them, and be done with it. When you're at rest, really rest.

"Finish every day and be done with it," advised poet Ralph Waldo Emerson. "You have done what you could. Some blunders and absurdities no doubt crept in; but get rid of them and forget them as soon as you can. Tomorrow is a new day, and you should never encumber its potentialities and invitation with the dread of the past. You should not waste a moment of today on the rottenness of yesterday."

Don't Worry

The strategies offered in this chapter should help you re-energize yourself, relax, and reduce stress. All of these things will drastically reduce the amount of time you spend worrying. Worrying saps your energy and rarely solves problems. Productive people spend their energy doing something about their problems rather than just worrying about them.

"Keep worrying in your life to a minimum," advises Reverend Louis Conselatore in an article in *Inner Realm*. His top three reasons to leave your worries behind are:

1. Worrying is futile and impotent. Studies have found that 40 percent of our worries relate to things that never occur, 30 percent to things we cannot change, 12 percent to health (while we are still healthy), and 10 percent to petty concerns. Only 8 percent of worries are about real problems. Thus, 92 percent of our worries are wasted.

2. Worrying is like looking at life through a dense fog. The total moisture in a dense fog 100 feet high covering seven city blocks can fit into a glass of water. If we see our problems in their true light, they can be relegated to their true size and place. "And if all our worries were reduced to their true size, you could probably stick them into a water glass too," Conselatore writes.

3. Worrying is bad for your health. A recent Mayo Clinic study revealed that 80 percent to 85 percent of their patients were ill directly or indirectly because of mental stress.

There can be a thrill in being super-productive—especially in a culture where busyness and accomplishment are status symbols. But watch out. You're not superman or superwoman. You need time to rest and recharge. Don't sacrifice long-term performance for short-term gain. Take care of yourself.

CHAPTER 13

MANAGING
INFORMATION
OVERLOAD

"We are now so preoccupied with keeping up with the bombardment of new facts, new developments, and new points of view that we have no time to listen to the past, or reflect on even the most recent history, much less to make a judicious reckoning of its significance."
—Regis McKenna, public relations specialist

As Richard Saul Wurman points out in *Information Anxiety* (Doubleday), more information has been produced in the last 30 years than in the previous 5,000. Everyone has too much to read and is drowning in data. A radio commercial for the Dilbert cartoon show has Dilbert's voice mail saying,

"You have 947 messages...all of them urgent." This is an exaggeration, but not by much. According to an article in *Men's Health* magazine, the typical Fortune 1,000 employee sends and receives 178 messages each day!

According to Reuters, an excess of information is "strangling businesses and causing personnel to suffer mental anguish and physical illness, as well as having a detrimental effect on relationships and leisure time." More than half of the 1,313 managers questioned in a Reuters survey agreed they needed high levels of information to perform effectively; one in four also admitted to suffering ill health as a result of the amount of information they now handle. Worse, 94 percent of managers do not believe that the situation will improve, and 56 percent feel that the future will be even more stressful.

Other key findings of the survey include:

- Two-thirds of managers report that tension with work colleagues and loss of job satisfaction arise because of stress associated with information overload.
- One third of managers suffer from ill health as a direct consequence of stress associated with information overload. This figure rises to 43 percent among senior managers.
- Almost two thirds (62 percent) of managers testify that their personal relationships suffer as a result of information overload.
- More than four out of 10 managers think that important decisions are delayed and the ability to make decisions affected as a result of having far too much information.
- One in five senior managers believe that substantial amounts of time are wasted collecting and searching for information.
- Almost half think that the Internet will be a prime cause of information overload over the next two years.

This chapter presents strategies for coping with this information overload. The key is to "filter" and be selective in your information intake, rather than comprehensive. It's impossible to gather and analyze all the information related to your work, and doing so would leave you no time to accomplish your necessary tasks.

Reduce Information Input

Many of my clients are newsletter and magazine publishers, and I spend a good part of my time convincing their subscribers to renew. But from a practical, time-management point of view, perhaps you should be getting fewer periodicals than you do.

The problem with periodicals is that they come when delivered, not necessarily when you need them or have time to read them. A book can be put aside on the shelf for future reference, but a periodical demands more immediate attention. Getting a lot of periodicals in the mail can be stressful; you feel compelled to read or at least skim them all. Therefore, you can cut your information overload stress—and reading burden—by getting fewer rather than more publications.

Here's a good way to determine whether you really need a publication: When the renewal notices come, ignore them and let the subscription run out. Then evaluate your life for a few weeks without the periodical. If you don't miss it, you just eliminated information overload from your life. If you do miss it, simply reactivate your subscription.

Many publishers give former subscribers (called "expires") a special lower rate if they re-subscribe within a certain period of time, so you are unlikely to be penalized financially for dropping your subscription and then re-subscribing later.

Don't Read—Scan

I get quite a bit of mail each day. People in my office building see this and ask me, "How do you have time to read all the magazines and newsletters you get?" The secret is this: I don't read it. Instead, I scan. Here's how you, too, can save time by scanning instead of reading, without missing important information:

☺ For many of us, the daily news has minimal effect on our day-to-day work. Therefore, it's unnecessary to read the majority of the articles and bulletins that cross your desk. I skip more than 90 percent of them every day.

- I scan periodicals for article titles that are relevant to my current interests and projects. Skipping the non-relevant articles, I turn to the relevant articles and scan them rapidly.

- If the article contains relevant and useful information, such as a good quote, an interesting statistic, a useful method, or an idea, I clip it. When cutting the article out, be sure to write the name of the periodical, date of publication, and page number on all of your clippings. This way, you know the source of the information if you want to use it later. Also, use a pen or yellow highlighter to highlight the one or two pieces of key information that motivated you to clip and save the article in the first place.

- After I clip articles, some are dropped into reference or project files for immediate or future use. If, say, I am working on a book about the Internet, I drop articles about the Internet I have clipped into that file. I also keep general files for topics I write or consult on frequently, such as computers, pollution control, finance, healthcare, and so forth.

- Others clippings that I find may be more of interest to colleagues than to me. I pass them on as a service. If I want to send an article to my colleague Ron Fry, publisher of Career Press, I write at the top of the article in pen "RF—FYI—Bob Bly." I then put a note on the article with the instructions "Mail to Ron Fry," and give it to my assistant, Carolyn. Doing so lets me correspond with clients and colleagues in a meaningful way. The best part is that it takes only a few seconds to make each correspondence.

- To avoid clutter, I don't save periodicals after I have read them. Instead, I throw them out (actually, I recycle them). If I need an article, I'll clip and file it for reference. You can also scan articles and store them on your computer.

Cut the "Info Fat" From Your Data Diet

Most of the information that you and I take in daily is a huge waste of our time. We do it either out of habit or because we enjoy it. If you enjoy it, continue to absorb it, but recognize it's a luxury and not a necessity. If you do it out of habit—for instance, your parents read a daily newspaper and watched the evening news every night, so you do to—consider breaking that habit. Doing so can save you a considerable amount of time each day.

Most of the information we're trained to absorb is largely irrelevant, both to our business and personal lives. So much news is either sensational or celebrity-focused—in a word, interesting on a gossip level but unimportant on a practical level. As journalist David Halberstam observes:

> We've morphed ourselves steadily from a Calvinist society to an entertainment society. We've become a less serious one—and a more coarse one. You can see this in the explosion of tabloid TV shows and in the changed agenda every night on the news. It's the power of images over words.
>
> When I was a young man, a great [newspaper] editor was someone who balanced what people wanted to know with what they needed to know. There's less and less of that all the time. The great sin these days is not to be wrong; it's to be boring. It's about ratings. Today, in fact, young people don't even read the newspaper.
>
> There is a stunning rise in popular culture. We've seen the "Hollywoodization" of our society, the rise of the celebrity culture, and the canonization of people who are not very interesting, are not very important, and have almost nothing to say, into major figures.

Gossip, celebrity, and news once were our fascination because following them provided an entertaining activity to combat boredom in our daily lives. Now that we are so busy, we don't have those empty hours to fill, yet we continue to obsess over the latest White House scandal or Hollywood marriage crisis. Why? Force of habit. Gossip, celebrity, and news used to be the means to an end (eliminating boredom); now they have become the ends in themselves. That's a bad thing for people who have better things to do.

The bottom line: Save time by cutting low-content media from your diet. Or at least make sure the content is useful to you in some way. My personal philosophy when evaluating information resources is this: If you don't think you'll use it, lose it.

Improve Your Listening Skills

The success of many of our business activities depends on how well we listen. Studies show that we spend about 80 percent of our waking hours communicating, and at least 45 percent of that time listening. If you are listening at only 50-percent efficiency, you are wasting 22.5 percent of your time.

Although listening is so critical in our daily lives, it is taught and studied far less than the other three basic communications skills: reading, writing, and speaking. Much of the trouble we have communicating with others is because of poor listening skills. "What I've noticed is that people not being good listeners, looking at their watch in a conversation or during a meeting," says etiquette consultant Sue Fox in a *ComputerWorld* article. "If people don't have the time or interest in meeting with someone, they just shouldn't do it."

The good news is that listening efficiency can be improved by understanding the steps involved in the listening process and by following these basic guidelines.

Are you a good listener? Most people are not. Sperry, a company that has built its corporate identity around the theme of good listening, reports that 85 percent of all people questioned rated themselves average or less in listening ability. Fewer than 5 percent rated themselves either superior or excellent.

You can imagine where you fall in this spectrum by thinking about your relationships with the people in your life: your boss, colleagues, subordinates, best friend, spouse. If asked, what would they say about how well you listen? Do you often misunderstand assignments or only vaguely remember what people have said to you? If so, you may need to improve your listening skills.

The listening process involves four basic steps:

1. **Hearing.** At this stage, you simply pay attention to make sure you have heard the message. If your boss says, "McGillicudy, I need the report on last month's sales" and you can repeat the sentence, then you have heard her.

2. **Interpretation.** Failure to interpret the speaker's words correctly frequently leads to misunderstanding. People sometimes interpret words differently because of varying experience, knowledge, vocabulary, culture, background, and attitudes.

   A good speaker uses tone of voice, facial expressions, and mannerisms to help make the message clear to the listener. For instance, if your boss speaks loudly, frowns, and puts her hands on her hips, you know she is probably upset and angry.

3. **Evaluate.** Decide what to do with the information you have received. For example, when listening to a sales pitch, you have two options: You choose either to believe or to disbelieve the salesperson. The judgments you make in the evaluation stage are a crucial part of the listening process.

4. **Respond to what you have heard.** This is a verbal or visual response that lets the speaker know whether you have gotten the message and what your reaction is. When you tell the salesperson that you want to place an order, you are showing that you have heard and believe his message.

When it comes to listening, many of us are guilty of at least a few bad habits. For example:

- Instead of listening, do you think about what you're going to say next while the other person is still talking?

- Are you easily distracted by the speaker's mannerisms or by what is going on around you?

- Do you frequently interrupt people before they have finished talking?

- Do you drift off into daydreams because you think you know what the speaker is going to say?

All of these habits can hinder our listening ability. Contrary to popular notion, listening is not a passive activity. It requires full concentration and active involvement, and it is in fact rather hard work.

The following tips can help you become a better listener:

- Don't talk; listen. Studies show that job applicants are more likely to make a favorable impression and get a job offer when they let the interviewer do most of the talking. This demonstrates that people appreciate a good listener more than they do a good talker.

Why is this so? Because people want a chance to get their own ideas and opinions across. A good listener lets them do it. If you interrupt the speaker or put limitations on your listening time, the speaker will get the impression that you're not interested in what he is saying—even if you are. So be courteous and give the speaker your full attention.

This technique can help you win friends, supporters, and sales. Says master salesman Frank Bettger in *How I Raised Myself From Failure to Success in Selling* (Prentice Hall), "I no longer worry about being a brilliant conversationalist. I simply try to be a good listener. I notice that people who do that are usually welcome wherever they go."

⊕ Don't jump to conclusions. Many people tune out a speaker when they think they have the gist of his conversation or know what he's trying to say next. Assumptions can be dangerous. Maybe the speaker is not following the same train of thought that you are or is not planning to make the point you think he is. If you don't listen, you may miss the real point the speaker is trying to get across.

⊕ Listen "between the lines." Concentrate on what is not being said as well as what is being said. Remember that a lot of clues to meaning come from the speaker's tone of voice, facial expressions, and gestures. People don't always say what they mean, but their body language is usually an accurate indication of their attitude and emotional state.

⊕ Ask questions. If you are not sure what the speaker is saying, ask. It's perfectly acceptable to say, "Do you mean...?" or "Did I understand you to say...?" It's also a good idea to repeat what the speaker has said in your own words to confirm that you have understood her correctly.

⊕ Don't let yourself be distracted by the environment or by the speaker's appearance, accent, mannerisms, or word use. It's sometimes difficult to overlook a strong accent, a twitch, sexist language, a fly buzzing around the speaker's head, and similar distractions. Paying too much attention to these distractions can break your concentration and make you miss important parts of the conversation.

If outside commotion is a problem, try to position yourself away from it. Make eye contact with the speaker, and force yourself to focus on the message and not on the environment.

⏱ Keep an open mind. Don't just listen for statements that back up your own opinions and support your beliefs, or only for certain parts that interest you. The point of listening, after all, is to gain new information.

⏱ Be willing to listen to someone else's point of view and ideas. A subject that may seem boring or trivial at first can turn out to be fascinating if you listen with an open mind.

⏱ Take advantage of your brainpower. You can think approximately four times faster than the listener can talk. So, when you are listening, use this extra brainpower to evaluate what has been said, and summarize the central ideas in your own mind. That way, you'll be better prepared to answer any questions or criticisms the speaker poses, and you'll be able to communicate with the speaker much more effectively.

⏱ Provide feedback. Make eye contact with the speaker. Show him you understand his talk by nodding your head, maintaining an upright posture, and, if appropriate, interjecting an occasional comment such as "I see" or "that's interesting" or "really." The speaker will appreciate your interest and feel that you are really listening.

Motivation is an essential key to becoming a good listener. Think how your ears perk up if someone says, "Let me tell you how pleased I am with that report you did," or "I'm going to reorganize your department, and you are in line for a promotion."

Once you've mastered the skill of active listening, you might wish everyone you speak to used the same tools. What can you do when you're the speaker and you want your listener's full attention? Here are a few tips:

⏱ Make eye contact. If you're speaking to a group, try directing your attention to various people in the room, one at a time. Make eye contact and speak directly to the person for a minute or so.

⏱ Avoid a monotone. Speak clearly. Vary your voice to keep people interested. An inaudible or droning voice can quickly put your listener to sleep figuratively and literally. By varying the inflections in your voice and speaking enthusiastically, you can command greater listener attention.

⏱ Ask questions. Whether they are rhetorical or demand some kind of response, questions keep listeners involved. When it comes to communicating, a two-way conversation is usually much more effective than a lecture.

⊕ Be brief. Don't be gabby. Get to the point. Avoid wandering off on tangents; stick to the subject at hand. If you are continuing a discussion from a previous meeting, summarize the main points and any conclusions that were reached, so that the current session can be more productive.

⊕ Choose a location with minimal distractions and interruptions. If your phone is always ringing, hold important meetings in a conference room away from the office. Doing so keeps people focused on the conversation instead of other activities.

⊕ Summarize and emphasize key ideas with examples and audiovisual aids. Examples help clarify your message and show listeners practical applications of your ideas. Slides, overhead projectors, blackboards, or photocopied handouts grab the listener's interest by helping him or her visualize your ideas.

Strong listening skills are vital tools to add to your collection of time-management skills. Use them daily!

⊕　⊕　⊕　⊕

More Tips for Handling Information Overload

1. **Be selective.** The Reuters report cited earlier in this chapter correctly observes, "People create and distribute because they can, not because they think it's useful." Desktop publishing, for example, has enabled individuals to more easily, write, typeset, and publish their own books; this has resulted in a flood of more books, but not necessarily better books. Look at the amount of useless e-mail—mostly widely distributed bad jokes—you get each day for further proof. Do not create or disseminate information or communications simply because it's easy. Only create information that achieves an objective—yours, the recipient's, or both.

2. **Subscribe to a customized news/data service.** There are a small but growing number of services that deliver "customized news"—usually via fax or e-mail—to their subscribers on a daily basis. One such "free" service is MSNBC (Microsoft NBC). Viewers who want more details on stories can get them on the MSNBC

Website (*www.msnbc.com*). CNN recently partnered with database giant Oracle to create CNN's Custom News Service (*customnews. cnn.com*). Also available free on the Web, the CNN Custom News Service lets subscribers set up a profile of the type of news they would like to read. Then, through a custom online clipping service, it sends articles and releases on the topics indicated. There is also a powerful search engine to let you find additional articles on topics not covered in your profile or clipping service.

3. Get your voice mail under control. Recently I was in a client's office as he listened to his voice-mail messages on speaker phone. As soon as a message began, if it was not a person he knew or not a subject he was interested in, he punched the delete button as fast as a mongoose striking a cobra. One way to save time in listening to voice mail is to politely but firmly request that callers leave a detailed message, not just their name and numbers. You can add that calls without messages may not be returned. Telephone tag is a particularly irksome waste of time, and it is inefficient. When you can't reach someone, don't extend the phone tag by leaving just a name, phone number, and call-me message. Say what you want and specify the response you are seeking. This enables the other party to respond fully even if he or she can't reach you personally and again gets your voice mail instead.

4. Reduce your e-mail correspondence. With time, e-mail users learn when a response is required and when it is just a waste of electricity and bytes. Avoid sending trivial e-mails such as "thanks," "you're welcome," and "my pleasure." Cut down on casual e-mails, because it will generate more e-mail—much of it requesting a response— in return. Lynn Lively, author of *Managing Information Overload* (Amacom), has another suggestion: Don't print your e-mail address on your business cards. "I give my e-mail address only to those I want to hear from every day," says Lively. Delete spam and other messages that are obviously promotional and non-personal. Ask to be removed from any e-mail transmissions or subscriptions you don't want, such as Internet newsletters or company bulletins from vendors and potential suppliers. When you send e-mail, write short messages; you will get short messages in return. When you want to end e-mail exchanges with another person, simply don't reply.

5. Protect yourself. Refuse to accept information input you deem un-
    important or irrelevant. Example: A salesperson from a store where
    we were buying new kitchen cabinets called to discuss some facet
    of our order or installation. I said, "Just a minute; let me put my
    wife on the phone," because the kitchen cabinets are her project,
    and she is the one who knows the details and is interested in its
    progress. But no, the salesman insisted on giving me the details—
    none of which I cared one whit about. Finally, Amy walked into the
    room. I cut him off politely, said, "Here's my wife; talk to her," gave
    Amy the phone, and left the room. "You don't care about this!" Amy
    complained to me later. She's right: I don't. I have limited time and
    too many tasks. I have to set priorities—we all do—and kitchen cabi-
    nets simply are not (and never will be) on my priority list.

6. To overcome this threat to your personal productivity, be highly
    selective in what you scan, browse, acquire, and otherwise take in.
    Limit your research and reading to a handful of clearly defined top-
    ics in which you know the investment in information acquisition
    will pay off for you. Jettison the rest or, if you don't, at least limit
    reading outside these core categories to things you truly enjoy.

7. Specify your desired content level. Frequently people communicat-
    ing with you give you much more information than you need to
    make a decision. This is a major time-waster and a constant source
    of annoyance for me. The reason people give too much information
    is they don't know how much you need. To cut down on informa-
    tion overload, tell them what you require.

8. Cleanse and purge frequently. Books, for example, become irrele-
    vant either because they're out of date or because the subject matter
    is no longer of interest to you. I go through my office bookshelves
    frequently, and my rule of thumb is this: Any book I haven't looked
    at for a year or more I automatically get rid of. (Usually I send it
    to a colleague who I think would enjoy it.) As information ages,
    its value declines (unlike real estate, which is often the opposite).
    Go through information resources periodically—paper files, elec-
    tronic files, books, reference manuals—and get rid of whatever is
    old or irrelevant. The reduced clutter will remove some of the stress
    caused by information overload. And, you'll have easier access to
    the remaining information because there's less to search through.

9. Combine information input with another activity. Standing in line at the bank is a waste of time, yet it is sometimes a necessity with no alternative choice. If you read a newsletter or business report while standing in line, you convert that wasted time to productive time. You can watch the news on TV while your family is shopping for a new CD player in the electronics section of the department store. You can listen to a lecture or a book on tape while you mow the lawn or do the grocery shopping. You can read a newsletter while sitting idle in a line to get your car inspected.

10. Know when you have enough information. When you're making decisions, don't agonize over the fact that you don't have all the information. You never will. Productive people develop an instinct for when it's time to stop researching and reading, and to start doing and acting. If you don't, you'll spend all your time in the library and not get anything done.

If you're still not convinced that managing information overload is critical to time management, try this experiment: Buy the Sunday *New York Times*. Start reading every word of every article and advertisement. Call me when you finish (I've got lots of time to wait) and we'll talk about how much time you've lost and what it cost you in productivity to take in that much information (most of it useless to your needs). When you learn to skim, scan, and choose selectively, you'll find you have much more time every day to do the things you always thought you never had time for.

Chapter 14

Saving Time at Home

What does being more productive in your home have to do with time management at your job? Plenty!

You have a limited supply of time—24 hours—every day. It is split almost evenly between work (1/3), home (1/3), and sleep (1/3). Therefore, if you can be more productive and efficient at home, that leaves you with more time available for work or relaxation.

You've tried to find minutes here and there to do your favorite hobby or even work on your own blossoming business, but it just never seems to work out! Something, or someone, always gets in the way—or maybe you're letting it get in the way! Now, you're so frustrated and you've lost belief in yourself because if you were "really a good at what you want to do, you would be making this happen." Right?

Here's the nasty truth! If you want this bad enough, it *is* up to you to take hold of your life, organize it, and control what goes on around you. Then you can do what you want to do. Like writing a book or building a business plan, however, you will need to design it. There are some very creative ways you can take to save time and energy, allowing you to fit more time in your busy schedule for your passion in life.

If a family is involved—husband or wife and kids—then realize that there are ways to reward each member for helping you out with chores and other things in life that you would like to give over so you can achieve your dream. It's all about building positive relationships with family members so that they want to help you reach your goals, just as you would like family members to reach theirs.

For instance, weekly allowances for kids are always good and promote the idea of being paid for working. If family members do more than their share, increase the allowance accordingly, or give bonuses for extra work. If it's a question of lack of money, consider other perks such as small gifts that are meaningful to each person.

We might wish that today's big corporate employer (or small business owner) would use this to achieve greater employee returns in hard work at the office! Instead, though most companies have turned to better customer service, it has come at the price of the worker who takes on more duties and responsibilities just to keep a job. Never mind getting a raise or bonus! Therefore, a business will have unhappy employees who really don't care about the customer, because it is not worth their time and they are unhappy in their surroundings. Lack of appreciation for underpaid workers will show eventually in negative net profit returns from lack of customer service. These circumstances can apply the same way in a family arrangement, particularly where children are involved.

For your significant other, offer to do neck and back rubs, or other small but appreciated gestures, to reward him or her for being tolerant and helpful. A special dinner for two, a small gift, or even flowers can go a long way to diffusing discontent and insurrection!

How do you even get started? Start with this first step: List what you do on a daily basis over a week's time. When you have created your weekly picture of what you do, then you can find ways to consolidate events or pass tasks on to others who will benefit from the experiences.

Use a Planner or Invest in Calendar Software With Alarm Settings

This is the best way to get started: making lists of what you go through every day in one place where you can see the whole picture at a glance. Also, you can add your family members' schedule and see how it all balances out (or not!). That will allow you to eventually work out a plan for finding more time to do the business or project you want to create.

Get the first week set in, and take a good, long look at how much of this repeats itself in the coming week. Start setting that second week into your planner and look at everyone's schedule again. There should now be a pattern developing, and you can start trying to consolidate events and household duties with family members who are available to help out. It is an excellent opportunity to start training children to take on added responsibilities and learn early on how to fend for themselves.

You can look to see when you need to make runs to the grocery store, the kids' ballet class, soccer practice, martial arts class, dry cleaners, gas station—you get where I am going with this. Consolidate trips on errands. Take someone to martial arts class. Then on the way back, stop at the dry cleaner and drop off the clothes, go to the gas station and fill up, then stop by the grocery store to pick up necessities you've run out of this week. In one run, you've taken care of three to four different necessary errands, and saved on time and gas.

Always keep a grocery list handy of all the basics you need so you can keep track of what you are running out of quickly. Add in extra specialty products at the bottom in pencil that you can erase when no longer needed. If you keep a running list of household necessities, you will be more likely to follow the list and not stop to look at other products not on your list that you don't need. This will help your wallet, too!

It may take some time to figure what will work best for everyone concerned, but without forgetting what *your* ultimate goal is: finding time to do what you want whether it be to develop a side business or a favorite hobby!

Here are some basic resources to check out for scheduling software programs:

- ⊕ *www.microsoft.com* (Find information about MS Outlook, MS Project, or any other scheduling software offered by Microsoft.)

- ⊕ *www.freedownloadscenter.com* (Search for Salon Calendar for a starting point. Salon is freeware, free to download. Look at other offerings, too, to see what might be a good program for you and is also freeware or inexpensive to purchase.)

- ⊕ *www.google.com* (Go here and create a free account with Google. This entitles you to create an e-mail address, use the online calendar, and share various documents with others online. Download the Google toolbar to easily access those features as well as plenty of others available to you.)

- ⊕ *www.thecalendarplanner.com* (Look at this software and check out side-by-side comparisons with other scheduling software on the market.)

Note: If you are planning to synchronize your new software with a wireless plan that can download/upload data to your computer, then check first with the wireless plans to determine what their software is compatible with before making the computer calendar software purchase. That will save you time, money, and grief from the very start.

Outline What You Do Every Day, Starting With Kitchen Chores

Sit down and make a list of the main things you have to do every day without fail. For a working mom, a typical schedule means getting up first and making the coffee. Then waking up the husband and/or kids so they can start getting ready for the day. After that, there's preparing breakfast and, while everyone finishes up and puts plates in the sink, you have to make the lunches the family takes to school and work.

Let's revise this scenario a bit. The night before, you fix coffee in the coffee pot, which has an auto setting that turns itself on in the morning. Voila—coffee made before you ever get up! You can also plan to get up before everyone else to get breakfast going and have a few minutes of peace and quiet before the crowd gets to the kitchen.

Everyone eats, and then each rinses their dishes in the sink and sticks them in the delayed-timed dishwasher. The dishwasher is set to automatically turn on when the first person gets home in the afternoon and then dishes will be dry by dinnertime.

Each family member then fixes lunch, finishes getting ready, and leaves for the day. When family members take on their own chores, then that leaves you more time to work with your special project, or maybe even make associated phones calls connected with your project. You will see in your events calendar where that time is showing up.

Maybe you leave first instead. Consider taking your laptop to work, where you can work on your project during breaks and the lunch hour. Be sure you have a way to keep your laptop secure (maybe locked in a personal locker, or stashed in a locked desk drawer).

Note: *Do not* ever use the employer's computer for personal documents and e-mail. You can get fired for misconduct, which also means you don't get unemployment compensation. Life will get rough very quickly unless you are already wealthy!

Here's another way to help yourself out, as well as the family too. For cooking the evening meals, invest in a crock pot, or maybe even two of them. There are some wonderful recipes on the Internet for slow cookers (Google "crock pot recipes") but buying a crock pot cookbook is even better to have handy around the kitchen for occasional study and recipe development. Whole meals can be cooked nutritiously in one large pot and quick additions, such as frozen veggies or dried pasta, can be added in the last hour of cooking for a final touch.

If you prepare all the food for the crock pot the night before, such as dicing raw carrot sticks, potatoes, onions and meats, and putting them in containers or baggies, then all you have to do in the morning is pull everything out of the refrigerator. Put each component in the pot, turn it on to low, and six to 12 hours later, depending on the recipe, and dinner is ready and waiting for when you get home. More time saved! Add a food processor and your time is cut in half, as the multiple cutting features do this job for you in half the time or less!

Along the same lines, if you serve salads often, then consider taking the lettuce heads, shredding or chopping each one, and put them in plastic bags for storage. Do the same with raw onions, tomatoes, green peppers, mushrooms, and any other compliments you use. When you're ready to create your salad, all you do is pull out all the plastic bags or bowls, combine together, and add dressing. No reason to slice and dice *each* time for a salad when you can get it done once at the beginning of the week!

Learn how to use the microwave, because an efficient one with 1,100 watts and up can do a lot for you in terms of saving time. Learn how to thaw frozen foods, cook different foods, heat up leftovers appropriately, and warm up that leftover morning coffee so it doesn't go to waste! Don't have a microwave cookbook for your microwave? Order one online from the manufacturer so you can learn how to cook with the proper wattage your microwave offers, or do a Google search to see if you can print the online version of that model's cookbook.

Another idea is to train the kids, if they are old enough, to take turns doing the food preparation on different nights. The benefit to this is learning cooking skills that will serve them well when they finally move out of the house years from now and need to feed themselves for the first time. When someone else is preparing the meals, you can schedule some extra free time for yourself to go to the notebook or computer to do some writing. You may need to supervise the first few times, but after that the kids will have it down pat. Always make learning how to do anything fun and entertaining. The lessons learned here will be invaluable later on in life. It is amazing how many children today don't even know how to do anything more than make toast or even a questionable sandwich.

If you are in need of replacing a dishwasher, consider getting one that has a delay timer, steam pre-wash cycle, soil sensor, and heavy-duty wash cycle in the control system. That will save you some time in rinsing dishes before putting them in the wash. Be sure to purchase a brand with a three-arm washer system that gives the best wash coverage from top to bottom. For most low-cost dishwashers on the market today, we still have to at least rinse dishes before putting them in the washer.

If you can, invest in a dishwasher that allows you to just add dishes without rinsing or soaking, thus saving time there. It is always important, too, to select any appliance with an Energy Star rating as that saves on your utility bills as well. Sometimes investing more in upper-end energy-saving appliances, such as dishwashers, refrigerators, and washing machines, will bring you money saved over a period of time. Keeping the noise down is also an added feature on upper-end dishwashers. Folks sitting in an adjacent den or living room don't have to be bombarded by the dishwasher noise. In fact, with a silent dishwasher, the kitchen table or bar top can now be used for you to sit with your laptop and write without distraction. No more jumping in your seat every time the dishwashers changes cycles!

Getting ready to replace your cooking range? Buy one that also self cleans. If you have ever cleaned an oven by hand, you know it takes a while and is rather un-pleasant because of the fumes and mess. Avoid all that and save some time by letting the range do the work for you. Other newer features for ranges are the ceramic glass range tops, which are very easy to keep clean with a ceramic glass cleaning kit available wherever electric ranges are sold. The trick here is to maintain the surface on a regular basis to avoid any buildup or hard-to-remove residue. Let that go too long and you will be spending much more time trying to clean baked-on food and even replacing parts that have not been kept clean.

Also, better-grade gas ranges now come with sealed burner fittings, which means no clean-up time of random food droppings under the range lid and easier cleaning overall on the surfaces. My quick-clean tip is to lightly sprinkle and soak the oven top with warm water, let sit for five minutes while doing other things, then come back with a soft scrubber sponge to get the mess up. For those hard-to-clean spots, grab a lightly soaped steel pad and scrub gently until the caked-on spots dissolve and wipe away. I also use a soapy steel pad to keep my stainless steel sink clean of stains and other spots. Just rub lightly with the grain of the steel sink until stains come up. Use a stainless cleaner and polish cream to keep your sink conditioned and easier to clean for future efforts.

Delegate Household Cleaning Chores

Family members can also help out with laundry chores according to everyone's schedules for the week. Figure who comes home when, and delegate two to three chores to each person. One child gets home at 3 p.m., for instance. So, that one can sort laundry and start the washing machine. While that is going, the same child can wash down the kitchen counters and make sure the kitchen is ready to work in for the evening meal.

A second child comes home around 4 p.m. and starts the drying cycles after each wash load is done. When the dryer is started, then dusting the upstairs main areas can be done between loads, by the second child.

A third child gets home at 5 p.m. and starts cleaning bathrooms so there is some semblance of sanity and cleanliness when folks get ready to take showers and brush their teeth. This child can also do a light dusting around the main living area just to keep things looking nice and not neglected.

Mom and Dad get home and begin preparations to get dinner cooking, or dished out on the dinner table if already done in a crock pot. This is a great time for everyone to start catching up with each other about the day's events and be involved in everyone's life. Too often now, families become distant as each person runs here or there, and there is no structured time to sit and talk about things that are going on in each family member's life.

This is only a sample arrangement of how a basic day can go. Needless to say, in today's world, there are all kinds of other things to be considered, such as after-school activities, late meetings at work, unforeseen family emergencies, and holidays that require extended family gatherings and travel. Everyone's schedule will be different, but with a listing of who does what during a week and who will be home at different times to do various jobs, those assigned issues can be worked out and rotated.

Making Time for a Green Thumb

Like to garden but find it time consuming? Here are a few time-saving tips you may not have considered. Use soaker hoses to water your garden. The initial set-up may take some time to get the layout just right for maximum water distribution. When it is set, however, here are some benefits of using a soaker hose system.

- ☺ Put system on a timer for early morning when the sun is not fully up. That allows the water to spread more evenly and soak into the ground before the sun gets to it and dries out the dirt. It's done automatically and you don't have to get up early—at least not to water the gardens! You can also set it to go off in the evening as well if the situation (high heat) and ground conditions (very dry) warrant it. Again, your watering chores get done for you whether you are available or not, and there is no waste of water if you've laid out your system correctly. It's all automatic.

- ☺ The soaker hose system eliminates potential leaf rot by watering closer to the plants' root systems rather than using a spray water hose, which leaves wet spots on leaves and flowers. When the hot sun comes out, the water, heated up by the sun, will burn leaves and flowers, making for a rather unsightly garden.

- ☺ On windy days, with a soaker hose system, it will not matter that your plants are still being watered, because the water is contained and distributed equally through a ground system. If you have to keep watering by hand-held hose, then you will lose a lot of valuable water to the winds that need to be going to the plant roots instead.

Keeping insect damage and disease down to nonexistent can be easy if you learn some important facts about companion growing. Trying to use insect and animal deterrents to solve problems can become frustrating, time consuming, and, on occasion, poisonous, if not handled properly. With companion planting, you avoid any poisons, and will be growing a totally healthy garden.

Find some really good gardening resources, such as *Organic Gardening* magazine, Rodale's series of gardening books and magazines, and any other reputable resource of gardening knowledge. Make a list of what vegetables and herbs you like to grow in the garden, design and lay out a plot according to what grows well together, and use other plants, such as marigolds, as a companion groundcover, which will keep away certain kinds of bugs from your precious vegetables.

The more you can make use of companion planting, the more natural and better off your vegetables and other plants will grow. Fresh vegetables from your garden can also be great gifts to give your friends, and if you don't have time to shop, well, your garden can give the gift that keeps on growing! More time saved there!

Go to these Websites to learn more about companion planting:

- *www.no-dig-vegetablegarden.com*
- *www.organicgardening.com*
- *www.gardenguides.com*
- *www.minifarmhomestead.com*
- *www.rodale.com*

Invest in a Family Plan Electronic Device for Full Communication Coverage

You were asked to outline your days and activities, preferably in a planner or calendar software like Microsoft Outlook. If you check with different wireless carriers, many phones and other small compact wireless products, such as the Motorola Cliq, are able to hook up to your computer and transfer data back and forth, like Microsoft Outlook calendars. The schedules you create can be shared with the whole family if each member has his or her own wireless device within some kind of overall wireless family plan.

If the family budget is tight but everyone has access to the Internet during the day, then check out Google for e-mail, calendar, and shared document capabilities. After creating an account with an e-mail address, you can create your schedules online in Google's calendar software that can be shared with those you choose. Although these features are considered secured, for your safety do not share vital information online, such as passwords or account numbers, that could be compromised.

Also consider whether the schedules you create will advertise whether you or anyone in the family is home or not, and when. Work out a way to avoid showing too much in that kind of situation. I use Google Calendar and love it because if I forget something, I can access my calendar anywhere and find information I've stored that I need in order to get to a meeting or prepare for one.

If you use the wireless communications system for the whole family, then it is easy to stay in touch, know who is supposed to be doing what at any given time, and communicate through messaging if something comes up and the schedule is diverted. You can also check to see if your plan allows you to "see" where your children are at any given time, a safety feature quite new on the market.

Check out the following sites to find out more information that you can study and see what plans might work best for you:

- *www.google.com*
- *www.t-mobile.com*
- *www.att.com/wireless*
- *www.consumersearch.com/cell-phone-plans*
- *www.verizon-wireless.com*

Set Aside Project Time and Make It Off Limits to Everyone!

Yes, this is free time you have set aside for your projects, based on that carefully worked-out schedule. Let no one mess with it unless it is a big emergency (like the house is burning down or someone has to go to the hospital)! If you are planning to make this a full-time business and career, consider creating some kind of goal-setting schedule. You can even develop a business plan that will help you take steps every part of the way to your final goal: a professional business owner.

It is important to find a spot where you are comfortable in sitting down with your laptop and you have peace and quiet. Some people like to play music or have the television running as background noise, whereas others like total quiet. You will have to find what works best for you and your creativity and your situation.

Do you like to have business and marketing reference books around you? Then design a corner of a room into a working area, if you can't get a complete separate room, and put in bookshelves holding all your favorite books sitting at your fingertips. Add a table with a good lamp attached or placed next to your laptop. Even though your computer's monitor gives off a lot of light, you will strain your eyes over time if you do not include a good reading lamp that sits just above and over the screen. Turn off your phone, sit down, relax, and get ready to start working.

Don't have anything to do or too many things you'd like to try but can't figure out where to start? Then Google different hobbies or interests that perhaps you might like to research, and study what's out there, just to get the juices flowing. Join common interest groups where you can make comments about blog postings, or even start a blog of your own. Having Internet access will be essential to marketing and researching for your project or business career, as there will always be a need to research facts and ideas.

Need Emotional Support Outside of Your Family? Join Online Groups and Resources!

Check out a number of resources now online that can help you support your journey to your business and project goals. Many resources will show you shortcuts and tips on how to utilize your time and schedule.

Here are some resources:

- *www.workingmomsonly.com* (A new Website with newsletter, created by former Early To Rise (ETR) CEO and Weiss Research president MaryEllen Tribby. Sign up for the free report, "The Decision Tree: Making Every Branch Count." This is a new site but promises to really develop on time saving issues and tips in future issues.)

- *www.earlytorise.com* (Another great Website for self-improvement programs and similar subjects of interest. Check out the news on finances and health, and sign up for any newsletters to learn more about what's happening in the world today.)

- www.franklincovey.com (Go here and click on the link for shopping planners to see all the products and programs available for planning and organizing your life.)

- *www.google.com* (Need this even be mentioned again? A great place to start to find all kinds of help and information on anything you need to research. Don't just stick with the first page of results. Look at several pages of Web links to find buried gems of information and help.)

Index

balance, 164-165

bad habits, 20-21, 86, 199

belief, 41, 58-59, 201, 208

BlackBerry, 122-123

Bluetooth, 129-1300

boredom, 24, 31, 42, 164, 197

broadband spectrum, 127

burnout, 42-49

chores, delegating, 214

cloud, conquering the, 126-127

concentration, 25, 43-44, 85, 110, 187, 190, 199-200

coworkers, 44, 47-48, 149

data, organizing, 156-159

delegating, 134-139, 144-145, 149-150

departments, changing, 48

desire, 42, 58, 97, 136

distractions, 21, 85, 110, 130, 200, 202,

80/20 rule, 21-22, 148

e-mail, dealing with, 130-132

emotional support groups, 218

employers, changing, 48

energy levels, 23-25, 85, 180-183

energy, production, 190-191

Facebook, 87-90, 95-98, 100-101, 109, 118, 126-128, 130, 172-173

feng shui, 183-185

fields, changing, 48-49

files, computer, 111-113,

gardening, 214-216

goal, production, 30,

goals,

      achieving, 58-59

      setting high, 34-35

      specific, 55-57

goal-setting system, 53-55

hard drive, 80, 108-109, 111, 115, 159

home office, equipping, 105-107

hotels, 62-69

info fat, 196-197

information input, reducing, 195

information overload, 193-194, 202-205

Internet provider, 113-115

iPad, 125-126

iPhone, 124-125

job, restructure your, 46-47

kitchen chores, 210-213

learning, 45-46

LinkedIn, 87, 95-102, 118, 130

listening, 198-201

mobile phones, family plan for, 216-217

Netbook, 108-109, 116

office, designing your, 107-108

outsourcing, 139-150

overwork, 43, 162

paper overload, organizing, 159-161

people skills, 145-149

perfection, 26-27, 34,

perfectionist, 26, 41,

peripherals, 109-111

personal assistant, 22, 77, 85, 134, 139, 142-145, 153, 196

planner, 59, 168-169, 209-210, 216

planning software, 167-178

pressure, 27-28, 58, 155, 162, 188-189

priorities, 14, 17-18, 74, 123, 153, 162-163, 204

priority grid, 57

procrastination, 18-20, 58

productive hours, 74

project time, 217-218

rail travel, 68-69

reading faster, 84-86

relaxation techniques, 186-190

saying no, 161-164

scanning, 195-196

self-esteem, 41, 44, 59,

sleep, monitoring, 185-186

smartphones, 119-130

    advantages and
disadvantages of, 127-128

    health concerns of, 128

social networking, 95-102

standard operating procedures,
22-23

10% solution, 71-86

thinking faster, 78-84

time, valuing, 36-42

to-do list, 14-18, 152-154, 156, 190

    daily, 16

    long-term, 16

    projects, 16

travel foreign, 66-70

travel, domestic, 63-66

Twellow, 93

Twitpic, 93

Twitter, 82, 90-94, 97, 102, 109,
118, 126-128, 130, 172-173

Twurl, 93

underwork, 43

value of time and money, 39-42

waking up, 76

wi-fi capability, 121-122

work

    asking for, 44-45

    enjoying your, 30, 35-36

    taking on different, 45

workspace, 25-26, 108, 136, 155

worry, 191

About the Author

Robert W. Bly is an independent copywriter and consultant with more than 30 years of experience in business-to-business, high-tech, industrial, and direct marketing.

Bob has written copy for more than 100 clients including Network Solutions, ITT Fluid Technology, Medical Economics, Intuit, Business & Legal Reports, and Brooklyn Union Gas. Awards include a Gold Echo from the Direct Marketing Association, an IMMY from the Information Industry Association, two Southstar Awards, an American Corporate Identity Award of Excellence, and the Standard of Excellence award from the Web Marketing Association.

Bob is the author of more than 75 books, including *The Complete Idiot's Guide To Direct Marketing* (Alpha Books) and *The Copywriter's Handbook* (Henry Holt & Co.). His articles have appeared in numerous publications, such as *DM News, Writer's Digest, Amtrak Express, Cosmopolitan, Inside Direct Mail,* and *Bits & Pieces for Salespeople.*

Bob has presented marketing, sales, and writing seminars for such groups as the U.S. Army, Independent Laboratory Distributors Association, American Institute of Chemical Engineers, and the American Marketing Association. He also taught business-to-business copywriting and technical writing at New York University.

Bob writes sales letters, direct mail packages, ads, e-mail marketing campaigns, brochures, articles, press releases, white papers, Websites, newsletters, scripts, and other marketing materials clients need to sell their products and services to businesses. He also consults with clients on marketing strategy, mail order selling, and lead-generation programs.

Prior to becoming an independent copywriter and consultant, Bob was advertising manager for Koch Engineering, a manufacturer of process equipment. He has also worked as a marketing communications writer for Westinghouse Defense. Bob Bly holds a BS in chemical engineering from the University of Rochester and has been trained as a Certified Novell Administrator (CNA). He is a member of the American Institute of Chemical Engineers and the Business Marketing Association.

Bob has appeared as a guest on dozens of TV and radio shows, including The Advertising Show, Bernard Meltzer, Bill Bresnan, CNBC, and CBS Hard Copy. He has been featured in major media ranging from the *LA Times* and *Nation's Business* to the *New York Post* and the *National Enquirer.*